HOW TO PLAY
DRUMS

Books in the *How to Play* Series

How to Play Bass Guitar
BY LAURENCE CANTY

How to Play Drums
BY JAMES BLADES AND JOHNNY DEAN

How to Play Guitar
BY ROGER EVANS

How to Play the Flute
BY HOWARD HARRISON

How to Play Keyboards
BY ROGER EVANS

How to Play Piano
BY ROGER EVANS

HOW TO PLAY
DRUMS

James Blades and Johnny Dean

St. Martin's Press

NEW YORK

Library of Congress Cataloging-in-Publication Data

Blades, James.
      How to play drums / James Blades and Johnny Dean.
         p.   cm.
      ISBN 0-312-08212-6
      1. Drums—Instruction and study.   2. Percussion instruments—Instruction and study.   I. Dean, Johnny.   II. Title.
   MT662.B625   1992
   786.9'193—dc20

                                                                          92-7231
                                                                             CIP
                                                                             MN

First published in Great Britain by Elm Tree Books Ltd.

First U.S. Edition: September 1992

10 9 8 7 6 5 4 3 2 1

Contents

Introduction

Drumming is fun. Nearly everyone has an inborn sense of rhythm, so why not develop *your* sense of rhythm in an enjoyable way by playing drums.

Drumming is one of the oldest ways of music-making, for 'in the beginning was rhythm'. Even reptiles and insects drummed: crocodiles drum on their empty bellies, and spiders drum on their webs to attract their mates. Stone Age men beat on great rocks, early hunters beat on their shields and tapped on their hunting bows, and long before the way to make a drum was discovered people drummed by clapping their hands and stamping their feet.

The invention of the first drum was one of the greatest steps forward in the history of music and the making of musical sounds. It was found that a resonant sound came from a hollow tree trunk when it was hit with a stick, and that an even better sound came if the open ends of the tree trunk were covered with animal skin. And that is how real drumming began.

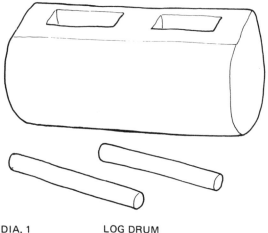

DIA. 1   LOG DRUM   AFRICAN KETTLEDRUM

In the beginning was rhythm, and rhythm is very much with us today. There is rhythm in the throb of a car engine on a motorway, and in the roar of a 125 diesel train. In jazz bands and rock groups we have the relentless rhythmic drive and exciting syncopation of the modern drummers who are the very heart of a band or group.

DIA. 2   DRUM OUTFIT

If you have never played a musical instrument, or tried to do so and given it up, this book will make you want to be a drummer. It tells you just how drums and other percussion instruments are played today and covers many styles, such as Pop, Rock, Classical, Jazz, and true Latin-American style. Every routine and exercise has been carefully planned by two professional percussionists who are also professional teachers. Their aim is to show you how to play drums in a manner that makes you feel there is a friendly teacher at your side. There are no boring exercises. From the beginning there are interesting and exciting rhythmic patterns which are explained in a clear and easy-to-understand way, and if you are not already familiar with musical notation you will find it explained in Elementary Principles of Music on Page 8. Music reading (an essential technique for the modern drummer) is also encouraged in many of the exercises.

How quickly you learn depends on you. Learn thoroughly and at your own speed. Do not rush through this book, but make sure you know exactly what is meant on every page as you go along. Take time to do everything the right way, and you will soon realise that drumming is not as complicated as it may have seemed at first.

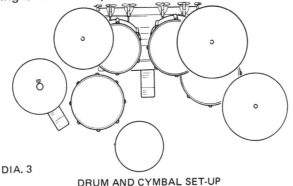

DIA. 3

DRUM AND CYMBAL SET-UP

Elementary Principles
of Music Notation

Music is usually written on five parallel lines called a stave. Bar-lines divide the music into short rhythmic units called bars. A double bar-line is used to indicate the end of a section, thus: or the end of a composition, thus:

Repeat Signs

There are several ways of indicating repeats. means repeat the previous bar;

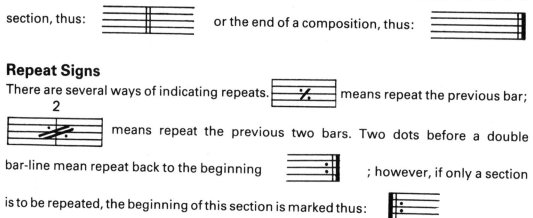

means repeat the previous two bars. Two dots before a double bar-line mean repeat back to the beginning ; however, if only a section is to be repeated, the beginning of this section is marked thus:

A repeated section may end with 1st and 2nd time bars. In which case, include the 1st time bar(s) up to the repeat sign. However, when approaching it for the second time, omit the 1st time bar(s) and go straight to the 2nd time bar:

At the end of a section you may come across "D.C." (short for "Da Capo") meaning go back to the beginning. "D.S." or "D.%" ("Dal Segno") means go back to the sign "%".

Indications of Pitch

at the beginning of the stave is used for low-sounding instruments, and is called the "bass clef". , the "treble clef" sign, is used for high-sounding instruments. Strictly speaking, music for drum kit requires no clef, but a bass clef is commonly used.

The actual pitch of notes in the bass clef are:

G   B   D   F   A   A   C   E   G

and in the treble clef:

E   G   B   D   F   F   A   C   E

Although most drum kit instruments are of indefinite pitch, certain lines and spaces are conventionally reserved for those most commonly used. (Properly edited parts will always indicate clearly which instruments are required.)

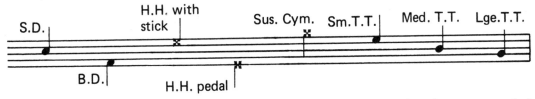

Abbreviations: S.D.: snare drum; B.D.: bass drum; Cym: cymbal; Sus.Cym.: suspended cymbal; H.H.: hi-hat; T.T.: tom tom (usually preceded by Sm.,Med., or Lge indicating small, medium or large).

Marks of Expression

Among the many expression marks in music, the most common show dynamics (loudness and softness): *p* - *piano* (soft), *mp* - *mezzo piano* (fairly soft); *mf* - *mezzo forte* (moderately loud): *f* - *forte* (loud) and so on. Observing expression marks is a sign of good musicianship.

The Length of Notes and their Equivalent Rests

The first principle of rhythm-notation is that each kind of note or rest can be divided in half by modifying the symbol used.

The longest unit commonly used is	𝅝	and whole-rest (semibreve rest)	▬
half of which is the half-note (minim)	𝅗𝅥	and half-rest (minim rest)	▃
half of which is the quarter-note (crotchet)	𝅘𝅥	and quarter-rest (crotchet rest)	𝄽
half of which is the eighth-note (quaver)	𝅘𝅥𝅮	and eighth-rest (quaver rest)	𝄾
half of which is the sixteenth-note (semiquaver)	𝅘𝅥𝅯	and sixteenth-rest (semiquaver rest)	𝄿
half of which is the thirty-second-note (demisemiquaver)	𝅘𝅥𝅰	and thirty-second-rest (demisemiquaver rest)	𝅀

To make sight-reading easier, groups of eighth, sixteenth and thirty-second notes have their individual, curled tails combined so that, for example 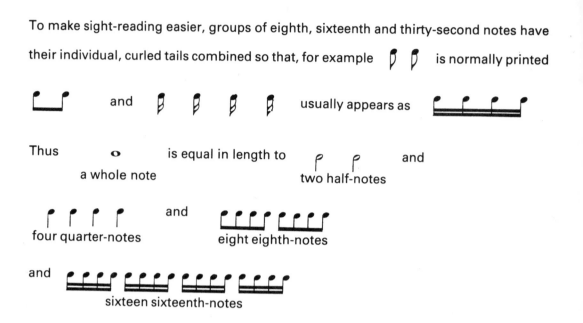 is normally printed

and usually appears as

Thus is equal in length to and a whole note two half-notes

four quarter-notes and eight eighth-notes

and sixteen sixteenth-notes

If a dot is placed immediately after the head of a note (or a rest) its value is increased by a half — a dotted half-note is the same length as three quarter-notes:
and a dotted quarter-note has the same duration as three eighth-notes.

A single note may also be extended by placing a pause sign over it. A pause sign over a rest has the equivalent effect.

Each rhythmic unit can also be divided into three notes by the simple expedient of printing three instead of two of the next smallest units and adding a figure '3'.

Thus is played in the same time as and is the same length as

This is further explained on Page 39 where these are incorporated into reading exercises. A system of abbreviation of particular value for drummers uses one straight line through the note-stem to indicate its division into eighth-notes, two lines to produce sixteenth-notes and so on. Thus equals ; equals . ;

equals ; equals and so on. Three lines crossing the stem normally indicates that the note-value should be played as a roll (see Page 32).

10

Time Signatures

The natural pulse of music tends to fall into regular groups such as the ONE-two-three, ONE-two-three of a Waltz. When music is notated, these groups form bars separated by barlines. At the beginning of a piece or section you will find a *Time Signature*, for example $\frac{4}{4}$ or $\frac{6}{8}$. This shows that there are four quarter-notes or six eighth-notes in each bar, with the upper figure indicating the number of pulses and the lower the rhythmic value of each pulse.

These are not however described as "four-quarter time" or "six-eighth time" but "four-four" and "six-eight" time.

Two of the various time signatures have alternatives: $\frac{4}{4}$ may be shown as "**C**" and $\frac{2}{2}$ may be printed as "**¢**".

Here are some examples showing the actual rhythmic pulses concerned covering two bars in each case:

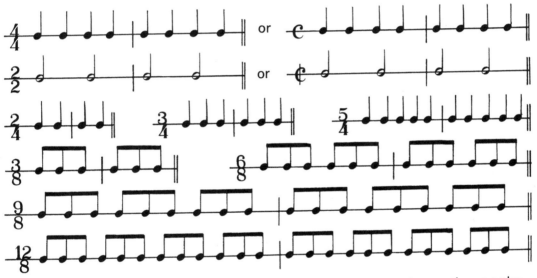

The following indicates how these pulses may be divided or notes longer than a pulse-value included. Remember that two eighth-notes take the same time as one quarter-note, a half-note is two quarter-notes long and so on.

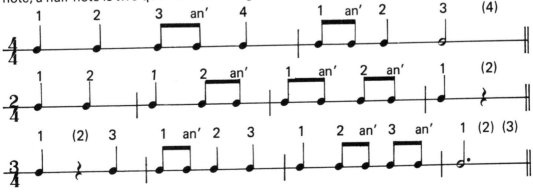

The Drum Kit

The Snare Drum

The snare drum, which until recent years was more often known as a side drum by reason of its being carried at the side on the march, is one of the most important instruments in a modern drum outfit. It is an instrument with a long and noble history. As a military drum it (like the kettledrums mounted on the drum-horse) occupied a place of honour in the regiment in peace and war. Calls to duty and signals in battle were given on the snare drum. Special beatings for the military drums were written over four hundred years ago, and some of these beatings remain in use.

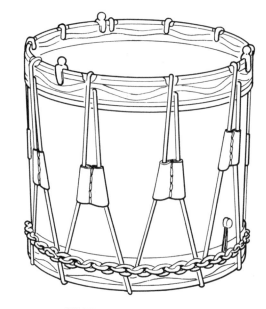

DIA. 4

TRADITIONAL SNARE DRUM

Old-fashioned drums were larger in diameter and depth than today's instruments. The shells and hoops were made of wood and the drumheads from animal skin (mostly calf) braced with rope (see military tenor drum). The snares consisted of gut strings which rested on the lower head or (more rarely) on the upper head. The drumsticks were heavy compared with those in present use. These old-time drums were used mainly in the open air where the drummers had tonal problems as the vellum heads slackened in bad weather conditions (these problems have since been solved by the invention of the plastic drumhead). As time went on composers began to include the snare drum in orchestral compositions, and for this purpose a shallow metal shell and rod-tensioning became popular.

(A large form of side drum is used today in regimental and marching bands, and occasionally in the orchestra. This instrument which is called a tenor drum has no snares. It is usually played with felt-topped drumsticks.)

Today's Snare Drums

The snare drum in use today with the drum kit is made of wood or metal.

Wood shells are usually made from birchwood, finished with a plastic covering, or the wood shell is stained, deep lacquered and highly polished.

Metal shells are made from steel, brass or aluminium. The brass shell is the most popular, finished in nickel or chrome plate.

There should be at least eight tension bolts to each drum head (see Dia. 5).

Drum Skins or Heads

The playing side of the snare drum is called the batter head, with the lower head called the snare head.

The plastic batter head is slightly thicker than the snare head which itself should not be played.

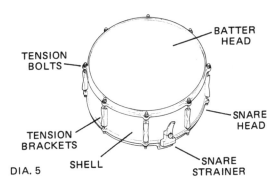

TENSION BOLTS

BATTER HEAD

SNARE HEAD

TENSION BRACKETS

SHELL

SNARE STRAINER

DIA. 5

The Snares

The snares which lay across the snare head are made from coiled wire. This produces a crisp sound with a good responsive tone.

Other snares available today are gut or silk-wound wire. Gut snares produce a solid tone and have a very different sound to the coiled wire type.

A mix of gut and wire snares is sometimes found in the orchestra on concert snare drums. The number of strands of wire snares varies between 10 and 24.

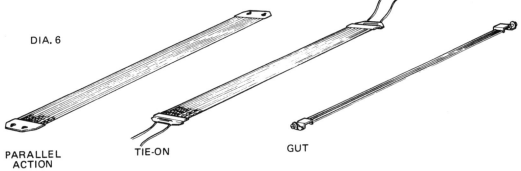

DIA. 6

PARALLEL ACTION

TIE-ON

GUT

SNARE TYPES

Snares are tied to the snare strainer or fitted to a parallel action snare release mechanism.

Internal top snares which lay under the batter head are used in marching and pipe drums for greater snare response.

The Snare Strainer

The snare strainer allows one to adjust the tension of the wire snares and also allows them to be released from the head.

Snare buzz controls are now on the market allowing you to adjust or dampen the snares to your required sound.

DIA. 7

PARALLEL
SNARE ACTION

TIE-ON
SNARE ACTION

Tone Controls or Damper

To control resonance an external or internal damper is necessary.

The external damper or control is preferred today, as this does not restrict the natural movement of the head. The downward movement is allowed, but the return vibration is dampened to stop most of the overtones.

DIA. 8

TONE CONTROL

The Snare Drum Stand

The stand for the snare drum must be sturdy and have ample adjustment for angle and height.

When using the traditional grip (see Page 30) the drum is played at the angle shown in figure 1 and for matched grip that depicted in figure 2.

You may also find certain rock players have their snare drum tilting towards them. This allows the player to play off the snare drum on to the tom toms with ease.

DIA. 9

SNARE DRUM TILTED —

—° AND LEVEL

How to Tension the Heads

Tension the top (batter) head gradually and evenly until the required sound is obtained.

The snare head should be a little less taut than the batter head.

As a guide — tension the lower head until you can just cause an indentation with moderate thumb pressure on either side of the wire snares.

For a meaty rock sound leave the batter head at a medium tension and use the external tone control or tape to stop any overtones.

As a rule the wire snares must be adjusted to match the batter head sound.

Snare Drum Sizes used with the Drum Kit

14" Dia. x 5" deep
14" Dia. x 6½" deep — Regular snare drums.
14" Dia. x 8" deep — Rock snare drum.

Snare Drums in the Orchestra

Various types of snare drum are used in the orchestra. They range from a piccolo snare drum 12" to 13" in diameter and 3" to 4" in depth, to a symphonic snare drum 14" to 15" in diameter and 12" in depth.

A symphonic snare drum is often used if tambour militaire (military side drum) is scored for. If caisse claire is specified a 14" by 4" or 5" snare drum is used. Alternatively a drum is chosen by the player (or conductor) according to the style of the music to be performed. (Other foreign names used for the snare drum include: *tambour petit* (French); *kleine Trommel* (German); *tamburo* (Italian).

Composers occasionally score for a tenor drum, in which case a drum without snares 16" or 18" in diameter and 12" to 14" in depth is used. When used in the orchestra a tenor drum is frequently played with snare drum sticks. If a tenor drum is not available, a deep snare drum (unsnared) is used in lieu.

SNARE DRUMS

DIA. 10

Snare Drums in the Marching Band or Pipe Band

Although the basic concept of the marching snare drum with regard to size and construction has not changed significantly over the years, the demands placed upon it by the player have, by comparison, changed quite dramatically. In satisfying these demands a number of important developments have taken place which in turn have led to the subsequent categorising of drums to suit certain segments of the total market.

A typical example of this is the pipe band drummer. Here is a player whose style requires a very responsive and sensitive drum, capable of producing a light, dry, crisp sound to complement the pipes and with the ability to project a very articulated type of playing. To achieve this a wood shell drum, capable of withstanding extremely high tension, and incorporating two separate sets of wire snares has been developed. By fitting one set of wire snares beneath the snare head in the conventional manner, and a second set internally in contact with the underside of the batter head, the characteristic pipe drum sound is created.

The Drum & Bugle Corps/Marching Band players on the other hand require a sound that is more rounded and full, but expect the same degree of response with more projection. Once again the wood shell, 14" dia. x 12" deep, will produce the depth of sound and projection required when fitted with gut or nylon snares, without any internal snare mechanism.

This is a very simplistic breakdown of just two specific marching snare drums, and does not examine numerous other finer details such as wood selection, forming techniques, bearing edge preparation, etc that are critical to providing the individual characteristics of any drum.

The Drum Sticks

Select your drumsticks carefully. The size and weight should be governed by the size of your hands and the style of playing you have in mind. A pair of sticks should be even in length, weight and balance, and they should both produce the same note from an object such as a table or desk (using the same hand). Test for straightness by rolling them along a flat surface. If the tip (the acorn) wobbles, the stick is warped — discard it. The butt (heavy) ends should be rounded off in case they are used when playing Rock.

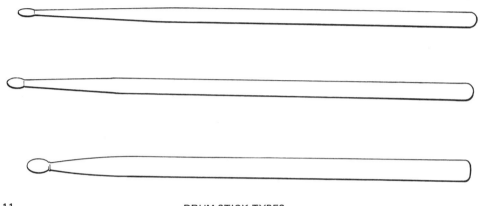

DIA. 11   DRUM STICK TYPES

The Bass Drum

History of the Bass Drum

Huge drums called temple drums were used over four thousand years ago. Ancient art works show Mesopotamian and Sumerian drums almost the same height as the player. As time went on smaller bass drums were used, particularly in Turkey. Turkish drums were similar to the bass drums used in present-day marching bands and orchestras. A famous drum called the English long drum became popular about 250 years ago. This instrument was a double-headed rope-braced instrument with a shell much deeper than the diameter of the (skin) drum-heads. For its size it had a remarkably deep sound. It was often struck on one side with a drumstick and the other side with a switch of twigs. Great composers like Haydn and Mozart occasionally used this effect in their orchestral compositions. Small single-headed bass drums called gong drums were popular for a time with early ragtime and jazz groups. Large gong drums have also been used in symphony orchestras, but today most orchestras use a large double-headed screw-tensioned bass drum (at least 36″ in diameter). This deep-sounding drum is normally played with soft-headed drumsticks and is usually mounted in a cradle. The largest bass drum in use today is said to be (Guinness Book of Records) the Disneyland Big Bass Drum. It has a head diameter of 10½ feet.

16

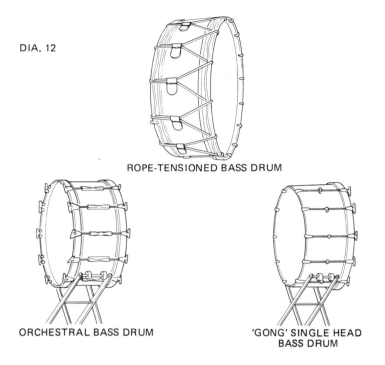

DIA. 12

ROPE-TENSIONED BASS DRUM

ORCHESTRAL BASS DRUM

'GONG' SINGLE HEAD
BASS DRUM

The Bass Drum in the Drum Kit

Big bands or concert bands require a bass drum sound with impact and projection. An ideal size is a drum of 22" or 24" diameter.

In a big band the bass drum can 'lift' the performance and keep the music swinging.

Play the bass drum two or four beats to the measure (bar), *BUT REMEMBER,* do not play loudly.

The bass drum should be *felt* and not heard by other members of the band (never cover up the bass player's sound with a loud 4 beats in each measure). This takes practice. You may be playing your cymbals, hi-hat and snare drum vigorously but you have to control your bass drum pedal and only play loudly for accents and brass figures.

Playing the bass drum in this situation may require a little damping to the heads. A felt strip placed under each head (Fig. 1), or a strip across the bottom of each head (Fig. 2) both work very well.

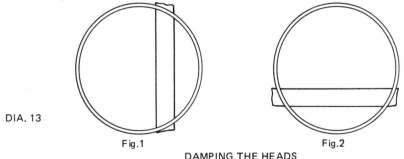

DIA. 13

Fig.1   Fig.2

DAMPING THE HEADS

Group and Rock Playing

In rock playing the bass drum requires a different approach. The sound is always loud and meaty.

The playing head should have a little give in the tension. You may find that a small patch of felt or tape stuck to the head where the pedal beater strikes it will give the drum a more 'punchy' sound.

The front head of the bass drum requires a hole cut out in the middle. Your Dealer will supply a head cut in the centre with a damping ring fitted to stop all the unwanted resonance. In recording studios it may be necessary to remove the front head completely (see Page 28).

DIA. 14

DAMPER PATCH

'POLO' HEAD

Bass Drum Sizes

18" Dia. x 14" deep	Small Jazz bass drum
20" Dia. x 14" deep	
22" Dia. x 14" or 16" deep	Standard size bass drums for Rock
24" Dia. x 14" deep	or Big Bands.

The Bass Drum Pedal

The bass drum pedal is a very important piece of equipment. The easy and positive action of a 'fast action pedal' is ideal for rapid passage work.

To achieve a good feel from the pedal — try the following:

Fig. 1 With your foot fully on the pedal.
Fig. 2 This is the kick action to gain more power and speed from the pedal.

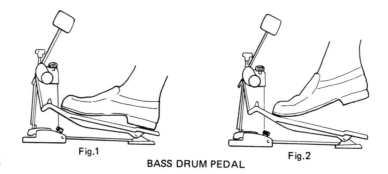

Fig.1

DIA. 15   BASS DRUM PEDAL   Fig.2

You may prefer to use two bass drums in your kit. This will require a great deal of practice to match the action of each foot, so that both drums are equal in feel and volume.

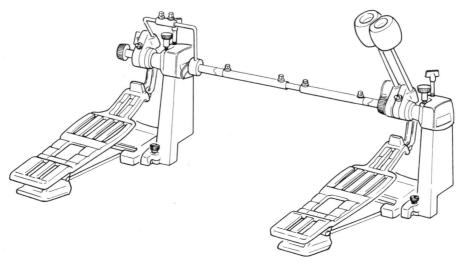

DIA. 16   TWIN BASS DRUM PEDAL

Above is a twin bass drum pedal. This allows you to play twin bass drum rhythms on one bass drum — very useful for fast passage work.

Double Drumming Technique

Before the invention, or general use of the bass drum foot pedal, the bass drum, snare drum and cymbals were played by one player who used a skilful technique known as double-drumming. The snare drum and bass drum were struck simultaneously as required, and a long smooth roll was played with no break when the bass drum was struck. The cymbals were played with a foot pedal known as 'low-boy' (Dia. 17). See Technical Exercises for a double-drumming example (Page 64).

DIA. 17   DOUBLE DRUMMING

The Bass Drum in the Orchestra

The instrument most frequently seen in the full orchestra is a separately tensioned drum in the region of 36″ in diameter and 18″ in depth. The drumheads are most often of plastic, though occasionally calfskin is used. This large drum is usually mounted in a cradle with swivel adjustment, giving a choice of horizontal or vertical positioning. The separate tensioning allows a difference of tone from each drumhead. This helps to render the pitch of the instrument indefinite — the sound required from an orchestral bass drum. The disadvantage of the once popular large single-headed orchestral gong drum was that a tight single calfskin produced a note of definable pitch.

The orchestral bass drummer uses several kinds of drumsticks, ranging from very soft to medium hard. The roll is produced with recurring *single* beats, as is the roll on the timpani. Due to the resonance of a large drum, note values must be strictly observed. The player controls the length of the notes by a hand damping technique.

The orchestral bass drum serves many purposes. In addition to marking the rhythm and strengthening dynamics, it adds colour to orchestral compositions — at times significantly, as for example to suggest a peal of thunder, or the boom of a cannon, as in the famous Overture 1812 by Tchaikovsky. Foreign names used for the orchestral bass drum include *grosse caisse* (French); *grosse Trommel* (German); *gran cassa* (Italian).

The Bass Drum in the Marching Band

Just as with marching snare drums, the expectations and demands of bass drummers have in recent years, dictated changes in the role and construction of the traditional bass drum. No longer is the bass drum and its player restricted to a simple 'Four in the Bar' with the occasional double beat to signal a halt or change in direction.

The importance of a good bass sound and a rock-steady player is just as essential today as ever, but the full musical integration of the bass line with the tenor drums and snares into the complete ensemble has led to the development of differing playing styles and the introduction of pitched bass drums.

Beater selection is critical to the projection of the drum's total tonal colour, with a variety of head sizes and materials such as lambswool and hard felt available to bring out the widely differing characteristics of the full range of drums.

Pipe bands in general tend to use narrow shell drums, say 10″ or 12″ wide, whilst bands using a number of tuned or pitched basses will choose a shell width that is equal to no less than half the drum's diameter.

Tom Toms

Tom tom is the name given to many types of drum, particularly to the native drums of India and China, which, like many percussion instruments have a long history. Huge temple drums have been used in China for 5,000 years and large drums were also used in ancient eastern warfare. Chinese drums were often barrel shaped, and had heads of pigskin which were fixed to the body of the drum with iron nails. Small drums used in theatrical performance are, today, still important instruments in Chinese music.

A traditional Chinese drum is easily recognised. The shell is painted red, and the two nailed pigskin heads are emblematically adorned, one with a painted picture of a dragon and the other with a bird (the phoenix, the bird of everlasting life). Chinese drums were used in early American and European jazz bands. These instruments led the way to modern kit tom toms.

Tom Toms used with the Drum Outfit are single or double headed.

Tom toms fixed on the bass drum are called rack toms or mounted toms. Usually the smaller size toms are mounted in this way.

SINGLE HEAD   DOUBLE HEAD

TOM TOMS

DIA. 18

The larger toms are floor standing. These may be on legs or mounted on low stands.

The normal set-up for a player to start with is one or two rack toms and a floor tom.

The drummer in today's group may have four rack toms and two or four floor toms.

Tuning Single Headed Tom Toms

Turn each tension bolt by the same amount all round the drum.

Over-tension the head and "bed the head in" with your hand. (Push the head down and round the drum, using a certain amount of pressure.)

Next, release the tension all round and tune the head down in pitch. When you arrive at a sound and pitch you like:

1). tune just one tension bolt down a little to achieve a slight bend in the pitch of the head.

2). do not use any tape on the head. Care must be taken to avoid a flat sound, so the single tension bolt tuning is somewhat critical.

Tuning Double Headed Tom Toms

The top head or playing head is tuned the same way as single headed toms, but you must tune to a slightly lower pitch for the bottom head.

DIA. 19

LARGE TOM SET-UP

Roto-toms can be used as additional kit toms. These are single-headed drums with shallow shells. They are mounted on strong adjustable stands and are tuned by rotating the drum (clockwise to raise the pitch), or by foot pedal mechanism. For timbales, bongos, congas, etc. see Latin-American section.

Heads for Tom Toms

A full range of drumheads is available for tom toms. Single thickness, see-through (transparent) heads, with or without a black 'Doughnut' sound controlling patch, or damped drumheads with two laminates bonded together.

On double-headed tom toms you can combine different heads on the same drum (on the playing and non-playing sides) for an even wider variation.

Experiment, when you have time, to find out which sounds suit you best, or have someone else stand and listen out front. The toms will sound different a few feet away and different again, 50, 100 or more feet away.

Tom Tom Sizes

Tom toms range from 6" to 18" in diameter, in single or double heads with different size shells.
Concert toms (Single-headed toms)
Power toms (Double-headed deep shells)

Timp Toms used in the Marching Band

In the marching percussion section the snare drum can be considered the soprano voice, the bass drum obviously the bass voice with the timp toms giving their support in the tenor range.

The majority of timp toms, or tenors as they are referred to in certain areas, are in effect single-headed concert toms carried in various configurations by a single player. They range in size from 6" to 16" in diameter and can be arranged on a harness in front of the player as a trio, quad or quintet of drums.

22

The most popular arrangement is a quad comprising 8", 10", 12" and 13" diameter drums played with either felt- or wooden-headed beaters.

Very often bands will use 3 or 4 players using identical sets of timp toms not just for added depth of sound, but also for the visual aspect of 6 or 8 hands moving very quickly in unison.

Orchestral Tom Toms (Concert Drums)
The large tom toms used in the orchestra are in most cases single-headed screw-tensioned concert toms. In the past tom toms were used in an orchestra only to give the music a native character, but in modern music tom toms are used to add rhythm to music of many moods. Great composers such as Stravinsky and Benjamin Britten have written exciting rhythms for tom toms. In some modern works as many as twelve tom toms are used. At times concert toms have to be tuned to particular notes, but in general the players adjust the tension of the heads to give suitable high or low notes.

Cymbals

Cymbals have long been important musical instruments in almost every country. The Chinese made and used cymbals over 5,000 years ago and there are many references to the use of cymbals in religious worship in the Holy Bible. The ancient Greeks and Romans used small cymbals as timekeepers in dancing and in religious and other rites. Cymbal makers were very special and skilled people, and they had secret methods of mixing metals which are only known to a few people to this very day. The type of orchestral and other cymbals used today were first made in Turkey by a cymbal maker named Zildjian (which means cymbal maker). Members of this family are manufacturing high-class cymbals in the U.S.A. and Canada. High quality cymbals are also made in Italy, Gt. Britain and, (by a family named Paiste) in Germany. In an orchestra, cymbals are most often used in pairs and the player clashes them together. Suspended cymbals are also much used and these are struck with drumsticks of various types and grades.

Kit Cymbals
Kit cymbals include suspended cymbals and the hi-hat foot-pedal-operated pair. They should be selected with the utmost care. Test them in every possible way for brilliance of tone, volume and suspension, and make sure the sounds are the sounds *you* want, particularly from hi-hats which should each measure 14" across, have a nice crisp sound when played with the tip or shank of the sticks, and bed down evenly to ensure a neat 'chick' when played with the pedal. At least two suspended cymbals are necessary in a basic cymbal set-up: a 16" 'crash' with a high-pitched fast response, and a 20" 'ride' with a full ringing sound and not too many overtones, which produces a clear and audible sound from the sticks.

Additional cymbals to the basic set-up could include an 18" Chinese (pang) cymbal, a small choke or splash cymbal (10" or 12") and a cymbal with rivets (a sizzle cymbal) — 16" or 18" for long sustain.

Cymbal stands and cymbal holders fixed to a bass drum must be sturdy, have large wing nuts for easy and positive tightening, and have height adjustment (stands and fittings are usually termed 'hard ware').

Repairing Cymbals

Cymbals are made from highly-tempered alloys, which make them brittle, and with age may crack or split.

A crack or nick in a cymbal usually begins at the edge and spreads towards the bell of the cymbal.

Cracks longer than ½ inch can be repaired by drilling a hole through the cymbal at the edge of the crack (see Dia. 20).

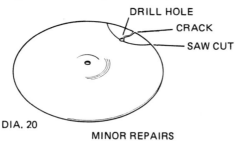

DRILL HOLE
CRACK
SAW CUT

DIA. 20

MINOR REPAIRS

Use a hacksaw to cut the crack out by sawing across the cymbal and through the drill hole.

De-burring is necessary after sawing or drilling because the rough edge may produce a new crack. De-burr the edge with a smooth file.

Remember that the repair is only temporary. A repaired cymbal may last a few minutes or more than a year, depending upon the nature of the crack.

If a large crack or split occurs in the bell of the cymbal, the instrument is ruined and there is no way to effectively repair it.

Warping of cymbals can be avoided by proper storage and packing. Use a good strong cymbal case.

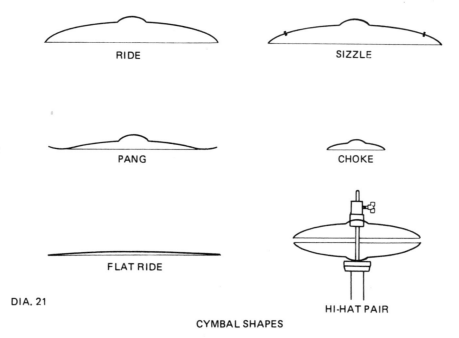

RIDE

SIZZLE

PANG

CHOKE

FLAT RIDE

DIA. 21

HI-HAT PAIR

CYMBAL SHAPES

Hardware

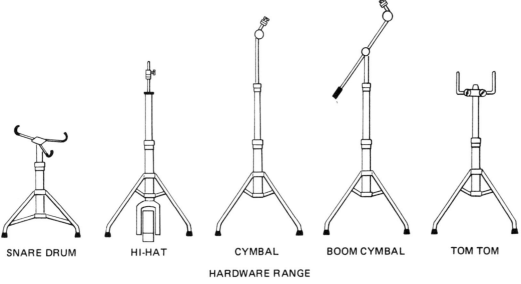

SNARE DRUM   HI-HAT   CYMBAL   BOOM CYMBAL   TOM TOM

HARDWARE RANGE

DIA. 22

The stands for your snare drum, cymbals and tom toms need to be sturdy and have ample adjustment for angle and height. The latest stands also have memory locks and a lead in for wing nuts.

Maintenance of your Drums and Cymbals

Clean all chrome parts occasionally with warm, soapy water and polish them dry.

Drum shells (metal and plastic covered) and all chrome parts can also be cleaned regularly with a soft duster and a domestic anti-static polish.

Lightly oil the threads of tension bolts, to make tuning easier and more precise.

Clean and lubricate the hi-hat and bass drum pedal mechanisms occasionally.

Never clean your cymbals with brass, chrome or powder cleaners. You will destroy the tone grooves and ruin the sound.

Keep the cymbals polished with a *soft* cloth and avoid touching them with perspiring hands. To clean a soiled cymbal use a *mild* detergent or a trade mixture. Rub lightly with a circular movement following the tone rings.

Setting up and Playing your Drum Outfit

Setting up your equipment properly at the start may save you a lot of time and discomfort at a later date.

Drum Stool

The height of your drum stool is very important. Setting this too high may cause discomfort because it places your weight too far forward. Try several different seat heights, and experiment by sitting at the edge of the seat or in the centre.

Find a comfortable sitting position so you can relax your upper leg muscles.

This gives you control of the hi-hat and bass drum pedal.

Snare Drum

Find the height which is right for you. Adjust both the height and angle until you feel relaxed with your hands and arms (see Page 14 Dia. 9).

Hi-Hat

Adjusting the hi-hat stand properly will let you produce the best sound from this important piece of equipment.

The spring in the hi-hat determines the effort required to press the foot pedal down and close the hi-hat cymbals. It also controls the speed with which the hi-hat pedal springs back to open the cymbals.

Adjust the tension spring(s) for your most comfortable playing position.

Different amounts of pedal pressure will create a variety of closed and open cymbal sounds.

Bass Drum and Pedal

Adjust the bass drum spurs for your bass drum height until your pedal feels comfortable. This will give you a different feel from your pedal (see Dia. 23) and help in controlling your foot on the pedal. Experiment with the tension on the pedal spring, making sure the beater comes to rest away from the bass drum head (also see Page 18 for pedal action). The beater should return to the starting position immediately after making contact with the bass drum head. This will increase your speed and control.

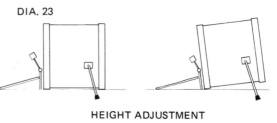

DIA. 23

HEIGHT ADJUSTMENT

Tom Toms

Place your tom toms so that your arms feel relaxed as you play. Adjusting the angle and height can affect the tone quality of the drums.

Cymbals

Don't set your cymbals up on stands or holders in the way your favourite drummer uses them.

The best angle and height depends on *your* size and the type of playing you are doing at this time.

Cymbals should be loose so they vibrate freely.

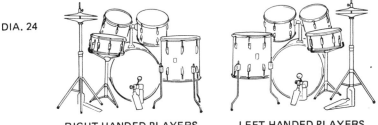

DIA. 24

RIGHT-HANDED PLAYERS   LEFT-HANDED PLAYERS

Important Note

Drummers who are left handed may set the kit up right handed. This will involve playing left handed (left hand for hi-hat, etc.) but may give the left handed player greater freedom for playing round the kit.

Drum Outfits in the Recording or T.V. Studio

Your outfit should be free from rattles or squeaky pedals. 'Mikes' pick up the slightest sound. Make sure the drums are not touching or they will make a noise by vibrating against each other.

Place your music stand where it is comfortable to read the music, *BEFORE* the engineer places the mikes round your outfit.

Always make sure the music stand is in line with the M.D. (Musical Director). This involves finding out where the M.D. is going to stand *before* setting up your drum outfit.

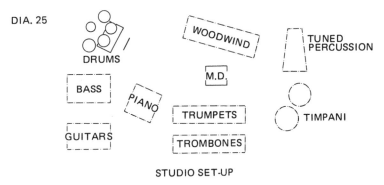

DIA. 25

STUDIO SET-UP

Your eye line will then be on the music *and* the M.D. for any directions he may give you.

'Miking' the Outfit

If you are required to take the front head off the bass drum, make sure each tension bolt box is taped up to stop any rattles from the fittings inside them.

Using 'Cans' (Headphones)

Most commercial records are made under very sophisticated conditions.

Usually the basic rhythm section (this includes the drums), is recorded first on multi-track recording equipment. The rest of the orchestra and voices are recorded later, on other tracks. The drummer is usually screened off from other members of the orchestra or group (see Dia. 25) for separation purposes.

Some studios have small acoustically treated rooms with windows facing into the main studio.

Placed in one of these positions, the drummer must always wear 'cans' in order to play "in time" with other instruments and also to hear the directions from the M.D. or Producer (see also "click track").

If the 'can' balance is unsatisfactory the studio engineer is able to adjust it by varying the sound input from the other instruments.

Studio Terms

You may have heard of the following terms used in the studio:-

Separation

To achieve the right sounds in the studio, the studio engineer must always have each instrument separately under control, so for example, he needs little or no sound from the drums to be picked up on the piano mike. For this reason the drummer is often isolated from the rest of the group. The separation of individual drums is achieved by using several appropriately placed microphones.

Balance

The engineer is required to adjust the volume of each instrument. This is not only for 'can' balance but for the overall sound of the group and the singers.

Tracking or Over-Dubbing

Using a separate track you can add another instrument to the existing ones on the recording.

E.Q. or Equalisation

If your drums are tuned to the meaty sound described on Page 18 the engineer may add a little E.Q. to each drum. The recorded sound becomes a little harder and gives more impact. E.Q. also cuts out some of the 'bottom' or bass frequencies from the drum.

Tuning your drums high in pitch will only cause problems for the engineer and the overall effect will be to make the kit sound like a set of high pitched bongos.

DIA. 26

MICROPHONE SET-UP ON A KIT

Click Track

In film music the arranger who has scored the music, calculates the timings in seconds or beats per bar. On the film session, each musician wears 'cans' to hear the beat or 'clicks', and plays the music to the speed of the 'clicks'. This way, the music synchronises exactly with the piece of film.

'Click' tracks are also used for keeping tempo and holding the group together.

Playback

After recording a piece of music the tape is re-played to allow the musicians to listen critically to their performance.

A Few Tips in the Recording Studio

1). To be successful in the studio, always be adaptable. The engineer or producer may require a certain sound from your snare or bass drum. Give them the sound they want and keep everyone happy. In return, your drums will sound correct for the end product.

2). It is important the whole kit sounds even. Strike each tom tom with the same strength.

3). On a multi-track recording session your kit will be balanced on the final mix. Be sure to give a good even sound from all of your drums.

4). If you are playing with one stick and one brush (as in a bossa nova etc.) make sure the brush stroke is the same strength as the stick.

Brush

Stick

5). TIME COSTS MONEY. Be sure to arrive early, allowing enough time to set up your kit before the session begins.

Drumming Techniques

Hints on Practice

'Practice makes perfect' is an old and wise saying, and if you follow the rules and practise the correct way you will find the early stages far from boring and, often as interesting as playing around on the kit.

Rule No. 1

To avoid unnecessary noise use a practice kit or at least a practice pad. The resilience of modern practice pads resembles that of a well-tensioned drumhead. Alternatively, use an unsnared drum or tom tom, covered with a duster. Position the drum or pad on a rigid stand at a height to ensure a relaxed posture, whether sitting or standing.

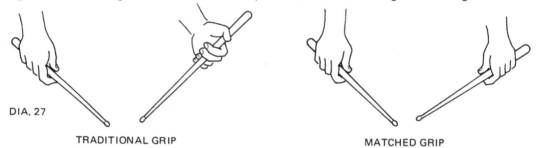

DIA. 27

TRADITIONAL GRIP   MATCHED GRIP

The Grip of the Sticks

There are two ways of holding snare drum sticks: the 'traditional' method, and the 'matched' grip. The right hand stick is held the same way in both grips: palm *downwards* and the stick held between the thumb and the first finger — the other three fingers control the position of the stick. In the matched grip, the left hand stick is also held in this way. In the traditional grip the left hand stick is held palm *upwards* and the stick rests in the hollow between the thumb and first finger, and is held between the second and third fingers. The points of balance are governed by the length and weight of the drumstick. The traditional grip is used if the snare drum is played at an angle, and the matched grip when the drum is positioned horizontally. Grip the sticks reasonably firmly. Too tight a hold will hinder wrist control. Experiment with both grips, and then choose the method which seems to suit your style and will best suit the type of playing you have in mind. You will find that the matched grip is certainly ideal for kit playing, and to be recommended if you play or intend to play such percussion instruments as the vibraphone or timpani.

Exercises for Developing the Grip and Getting the Feel of the Instrument
The first step
Strike the drum or pad in the centre with a direct blow, avoiding a circular movement, particularly in the left hand. Use wrist action lifting the sticks clear of the drum after every stroke. Make each stroke the same sound and strength by using controlled wrist movement and lifting each stick the same height from the drum (keep your elbows slightly clear of your body and while it is natural to look down at the drum when practising, do not make this a habit).

At a slow tempo (one beat per second). Signified ♩=60—60 crotchets per minute.
R = Right hand; L = Left hand.

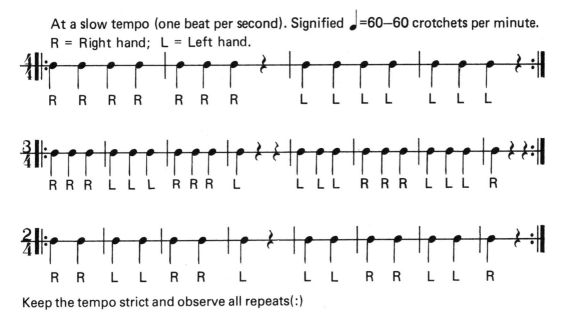

Keep the tempo strict and observe all repeats(:)

Use the quarter note rests for reflection.

Single Sticking

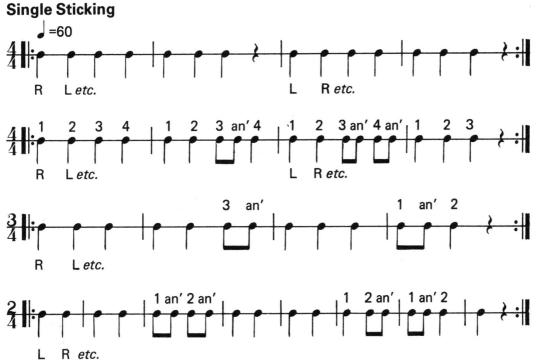

When practising these exercises you can use them as elementary reading exercises by
saying: one — two — three — four, etc.

Double Sticking

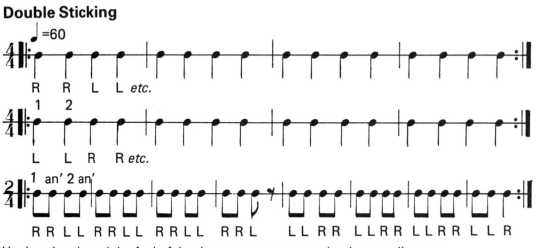

Having developed the feel of the drum we move on to the drum rudiments.

The Rudiments

The roll — indicated  Trem. The roll is the drummer's sustained note. It consists of an uninterrupted series of beats, free of rhythmic stresses, and played at a speed to give the effect of continuity.

There is no satisfactory short cut to developing the roll

The Double Beat Roll (the Dad-dy, Mam-my roll)

Practise slowly and *gradually* accelerate — a technique known as closing the roll.

Exercise 1

With practice the beatings will gain speed and at a certain speed you will find that the second stroke begins to fall more easily, and builds up to a double bounce from one stroke of the drumstick. Make sure the beats remain even. If they start to 'dither', stop and make a fresh start.

'Doubling the Doubles'

Exercise 2

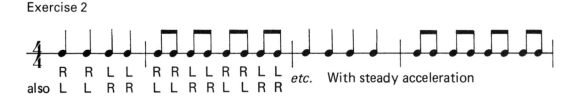

Exercise 2 is a good exercise for correcting any faults that may occur in a double speed bar as the slow strokes which follow allow time for mental reflection. Time spent on developing a good smooth roll is time well spent — a drummer is often judged by his roll and, of course, by his sense of rhythm.

The Stroke Rolls

The practising of the long roll can be assisted by giving time to certain of the short rolls, such as the five-stroke, the seven-stroke, and the nine-stroke.

Examples: Five-, Seven- and Nine-Stroke Rolls

Exercise 3 (Make as many repeats as you wish — technical term: repeat ad lib).

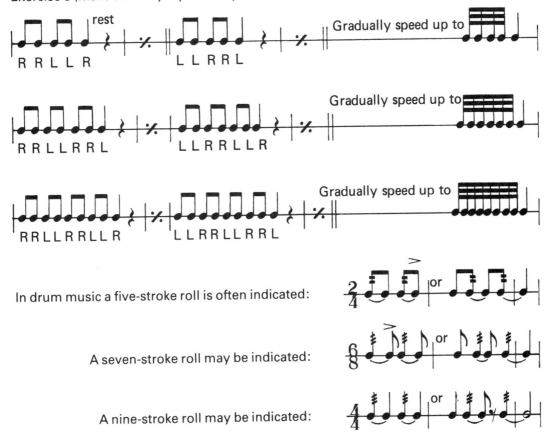

Finish each of the stroke rolls with a clean stroke, but make no accent unless marked.

Note that these rolls are carried on to the last note with a curved line ‿‿‿ : a Tie. (It must be remembered however that the tempo governs the length of notes in all time values — no hard and fast rule can be laid down as to the number of strokes in *any* roll.)

The Single Stroke Roll

The single stroke roll is a modern technique if compared with the long usage of the traditional double stroke roll. It is however an important addition to the drum rudiments and can be used to good effect in modern drumming.

The single stroke roll is produced by rapidly repeated single beats and the exercises for the double stroke roll all apply to the single stroke roll. There are also the 'buzz' or press roll and the multiple bounce roll. In the buzz or press roll a slight buzz is made on each of the rapidly repeated single beats, and the sound produced somewhat resembles a close double beat roll. The multiple bounce roll consists of three or more bounces with each hand.

These modern rolls can be used as desired, particularly when a roll is to be played at pp level. They can also be used until the true Daddy Mammy roll is considered secure.

DIA. 28

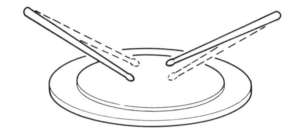

'BUZZ' STROKE

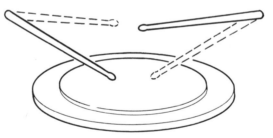

SINGLE STROKE

Grace Notes (Ornaments)

The principal grace notes used in modern drumming are the flam, the drag, and the ruff. The flam is a combination of a grace note preceding the main note — notated

♪♩ or ♩ .The grace note is played lightly and immediately before the main note.

Tonally a flam is best produced if the stick playing the main note is lifted higher than the stick playing the grace note.

Flams (and all grace notes) must be practised with a start from either hand, and until a series of them can be played in strict tempo.

34

Flam Exercises

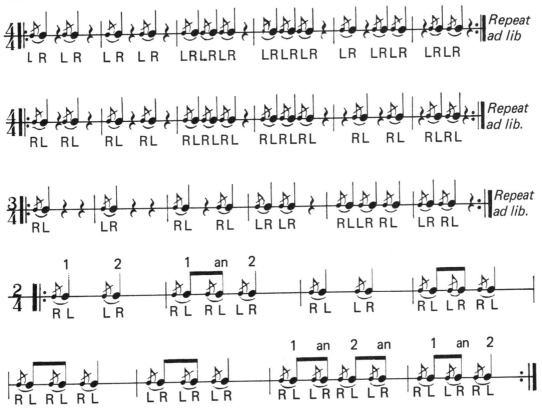

The Drag

A drag — notated ♪♩ or ♪♩ — is a combination of *two* light (bouncing) beats played with one stick before the main note. To avoid delay on the main note it must immediately follow the two light beats. Execute as the flam, lifting the stick playing the main note the higher. Make sure you use a relaxed grip with finger control particularly for the bouncing beats.

Drag Exercises

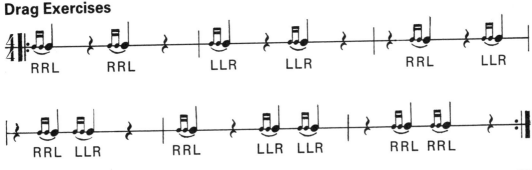

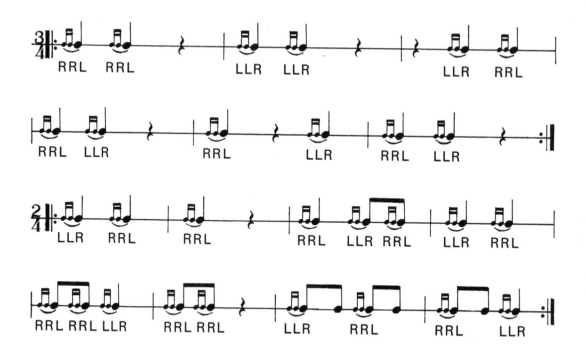

Repeat the flam and drag exercises many times — starting *slowly*. Are you keeping a strict tempo in each exercise, observing the rests correctly, and counting the one-and-two etc. rhythmically?

The Ruff

The rudimental sticking of the ruff is from hand to hand with a slight accent on the last stroke ![notation] or ![notation] The ruff can be used effectively in modern drumming
LR LR   R LR L

as a close triplet preceding a main note.

Alternative stickings (with bouncings). ![notation], ![notation], ![notation], ![notation].
RRLR   LLR L   RLLR   LRRL

The Paradiddle

The paradiddle is one of the most important of the basic drum rudiments. It is also one of the most useful, being particularly applicable to modern drumming methods.

The single paradiddle

R L R R L R L L R L R R L R L L R L R R L R L L

The double paradiddle

R L R L R R L R L R L L R L R L R R L R L R L L

The triple paradiddle

R L R L R L R R L R L R L R L L R L R L R L R R

The stroke paradiddle

R L R R L R L L R L R R L R L L R L R R L R L L

The flam paradiddle

LR L R R RL R L L LR L R R RL R L L LR L R R RL R L L

The drag paradiddle

LLR L R R RRL R L L LLR L R RRL R L L LLR L R RRL R L L

37

Double Paradiddle in Triplet for Drum Out-Fit

R L R L R R L R L R L L   R L R L R L R R L R L R L L

R L R L R R L   L R L   R L L R

Add Bass Drum

R L R L >> L R L R >>   R L R L >> L R L R >>

R > R > R R L > L > L L   R > R > R R L > L > L L

Triple Paradiddle with Bass Drum

R L R L R L R L R R L R L R   L R L L

R L R L R L >>   R L R L R L >>

L > L > L > L L   R > R > R > R R

R > R > R > R R > L > L > L > L L >

38

The Ratamacue

The single ratamacue consists of a triplet followed by a single stroke. A grace note

(♫) is played ahead of the triplet

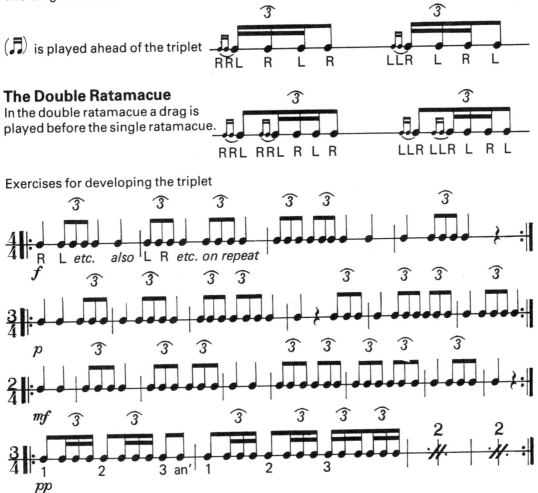

The Double Ratamacue

In the double ratamacue a drag is played before the single ratamacue.

Exercises for developing the triplet

Exercise 4 is the snare drum part from the famous *Bolero* by Ravel. The two-bar pattern is played 165 times with a steady crescendo, the first 4 bars being *solo*. (Play at ♩ = 100)

Try out some simple rudiments on your drum out-fit. Experiment with various permutations around your tom toms and bass drum.

Take a single ratamacue on a snare drum or practice pad, this sounds very military.

The same ratamacue around your kit has a swinging effect.

BASICS WITHOUT TEARS
(Singles, Doubles and Paradiddles — played round the kit)

Small tom

Medium tom

Floor tom

(1) Singles

R L etc, also L R etc.

(2) Doubles

R R L L etc, also L L R R etc.

(3) Singles and Doubles (♪♪♪♪ Singles, ♪♪♪♪ Doubles)

R L R L R R L L etc.

(4) Paradiddles

R L R R L R L L   R L R R L R L L   R L R R L R L L   R L R R L R L L

L R L L R L R R   L R L L R L R R   L R L L R L R R   L R L L R

Eyes skinned — now paradiddles with a start on the *left* hand.

40

'The Mix-up' (Singles, Doubles and Paradiddles).

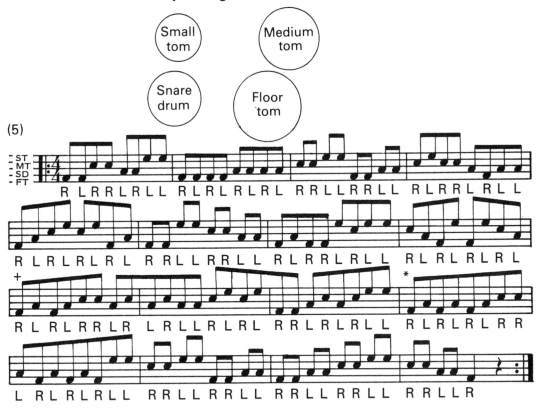

(5)

R L R R L R L L   R L R L R L R L   R R L L R R L L   R L R R L R L L

R L R L R L R L   R R L L R R L L   R L R R L R L L   R L R L R L R L

+

R L R L R R L R   L R L L R L R L   R R L R L R L L   R L R L R L R R

*

L R L R L R L L   R R L L R R L L   R R L L R R L L   R R L L R

+ Bars 9, 10 and 11 are played as consecutive double paradiddles

*Bars 11 and 12 are played as consecutive triple paradiddles

Play Exercises (1) to (5) at a slow and rigid tempo (♩ = 60). Practise until *all* the exercises can be played in strict tempo at ♩ = 120. When Exercise (5) is 'under your fingers' play it at three dynamic levels p - mf - f.

Now *you* compose a paradiddle piece and a 'mix-up'.

The Next Step

Progressive Exercises for the Snare Drum

The practising of the following progressive exercises and routines for the snare drum will not only lead to a sound technique and the ability to read well on this most important instrument, it will also pave the way to a good all-round performance on the drum kit. Many of these examples can be applied to the drum kit, and you will find that as your technique and reading advances, your drumming skills and powers of musicianly improvisation will forge ahead accordingly.

Examples 1, 2 and 3 are designed to polish up some of the early rudiments while playing interesting patterns. They are also planned to develop rhythm control. Keep a strict tempo in *all* your exercises and you will always hold the tempo in a group.

(1)   Play this exercise in strict tempo — if possible to a metronome set at ♩ = 100 Note how the eighth and sixteenth notes are broken down to read easily.

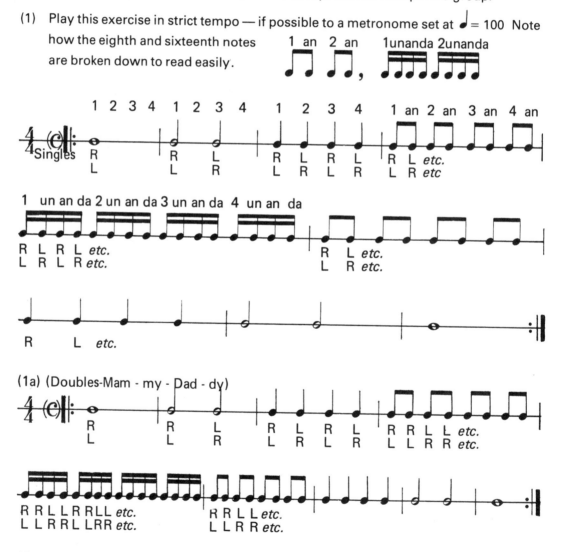

(1b) (Paradiddles)

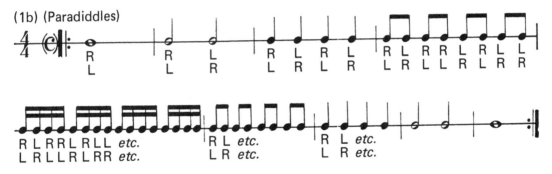

R L R R L R L L *etc.*
L R L L R L R R *etc.*

R L *etc.*
L R *etc.*

R L *etc.*
L R *etc.*

Exercise 2 is the same as Exercise 1 but played on the drum kit (floor tom, snare drum, medium tom, small tom).

(2)

ST
MT
SD
FT

R

R L R L R L

R R L L R R L L

R L R R L R L L R R L L R R L L R R L L R L R L R L R

A simple exercise in common time (watch mf and p).

(3)

mf

p

The rhythm of Exercise 3, with rests. Make sure you count the rests in strict time.

(4)

p

mf

In Exercise 5 we have 'one-anda' and 'two-un-an' etc. Say these speech rhythms as you play them.

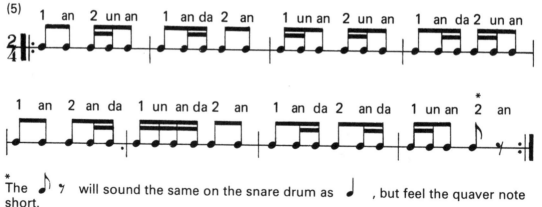

The ♪ ⅞ will sound the same on the snare drum as ♩ , but feel the quaver note short.
(On an orchestral bass drum or the timpani, you would 'hand damp' the last quaver* to shorten)

Exercise 6 is in **2/4** time, with an 'off beat' (oom-pah) rhythm.

Play this exercise right left, or left right, with the off beats played with the same hand whilst the other hand moves silently *on* the beat.

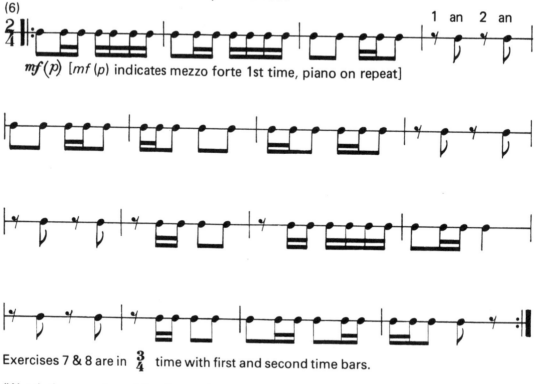

Exercises 7 & 8 are in **3/4** time with first and second time bars.

(Watch those rests and the first and second time bars.)

44

(7)

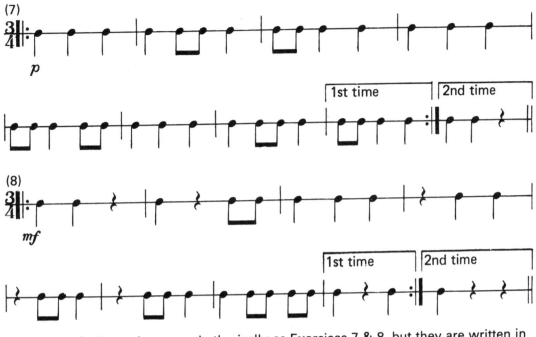

p

1st time | 2nd time

(8)

mf

1st time | 2nd time

Exercises 9 & 10 are the same rhythmically as Exercises 7 & 8, but they are written in $\frac{3}{8}$ time — three quavers in a bar. Play Exercises 7 & 8 ♩ = 60 and practise Exercises 9 & 10 until you can play them (whilst relaxed) at ♩ = 120.

(9)

1   2   3   1   2   an   3

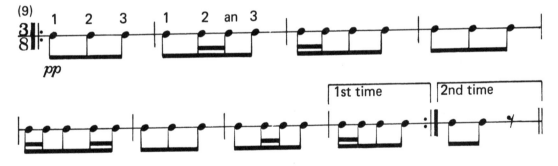

pp

1st time | 2nd time

(10)

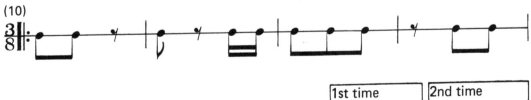

1st time | 2nd time

The exercises in $\frac{3}{8}$ time lead well to $\frac{6}{8}$ time (six quavers in a bar). First play this exercise at a very steady tempo and finally at a faster speed. Do not speed up *during* an exercise. For the dotted crotchet etc. first count:

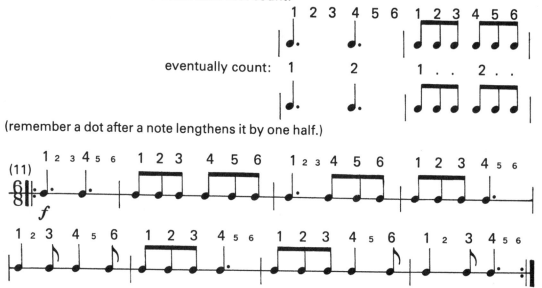

eventually count:

(remember a dot after a note lengthens it by one half.)

(11)

Exercises 11, 12, 13 and 14 are in compound time, the name given to time signatures with a dotted-note pulse. Practise as follows: Exercises 11, 12 and 13 with a two pulse feel; Exercise 14 with a three pulse feel changing to a four pulse feel. $\frac{6}{8}$, $\frac{9}{8}$ and $\frac{12}{8}$ are frequently played at too fast a speed to count every quaver.

Exercise 12 is as Exercise 11 with bars 5-7 and 8 written in a different way.

You will soon learn to cope with the several ways of writing drum music.

In this example we introduce the flam.

(12)

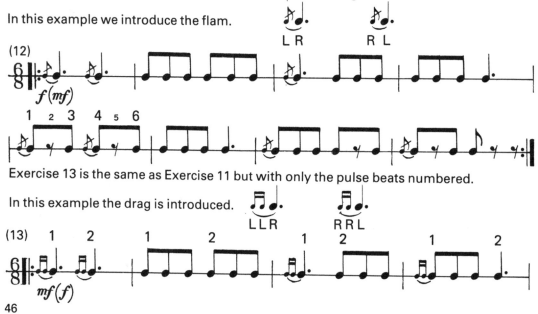

Exercise 13 is the same as Exercise 11 but with only the pulse beats numbered.

In this example the drag is introduced.

(13)

46

Exercise 14 is in $\frac{9}{8}$ time changing to $\frac{12}{8}$ time. Be sure to keep the tempo rigid when the time signature changes at bar 5.

(14) 1 2 3 4 5 6 7 8 9   1 2 3 4 5 6 7 8 9   1 . . 2 . . 3 . . 1 . . 2 . . 3 . .

cresc.

1 . . 2 . . 3 . . 4 . .

We now have two examples using triplets (three quavers in the time of one crotchet.)

(Semiquaver triplets and tied notes etc. are dealt with in the advanced exercises.)

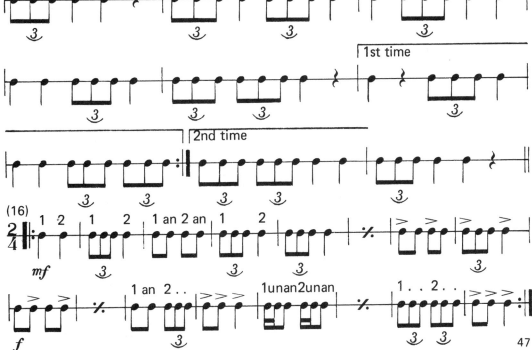

(15)

1 2 3 4   1 2 an a 3 4 an a

1st time

2nd time

(16) 1 2   1 2   1 an 2 an   1 2

1 an 2 . .   1unan2unan   1 . . 2 . .

Exercise 17. An exercise with accents, diminuendos and crescendos.

This exercise is in ¢ time (alla breve or 'cut common'). Though it is written in $\frac{4}{4}$ time feel a 'two in a bar' pulse.

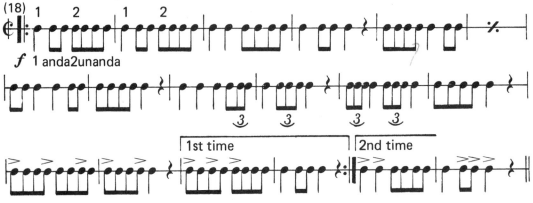

This is a preparatory exercise for the application of the roll. Note that some of the rolls are tied to the following note and some are *not* tied. Where there is no tie cease the roll

a fraction before the next beat. In bar 18 for example play ⚎ not ⚎

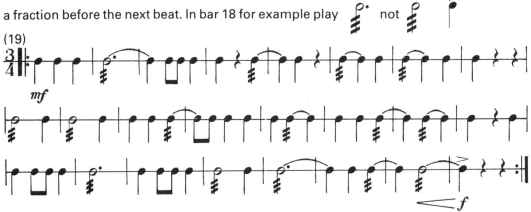

When sight reading an exercise it may be found that playing hand to hand (R L or L R etc) is safer. When familiar with the piece use singles, double beats or a paradiddle to suit your style.

48

Sight Reading Music for the Drum Kit (Rock etc.)

The eyes of the drummer must be trained to see whole patterns and phrases, not just individual snare drum, bass drum or cymbal lines.

Exercises 1 to 6 involve bass drum, snare drum and hi-hat.

The hi-hat is now played with your right hand stick. Keep your hi-hat pedal closed with your foot down on the pedal. No snare drum is needed.

Open the cymbals slightly when you see this sign ⊗ by taking some pressure off the pedal.

The following exercises continue with the hi-hat, but with different bass drum notations for co-ordination between hands and feet.

Play slowly at first keeping strict time within each exercise.

The next two exercises are in $\frac{3}{4}$ time.

Keep the rhythm flowing and in time.

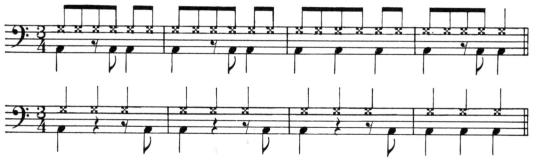

DIA. 29

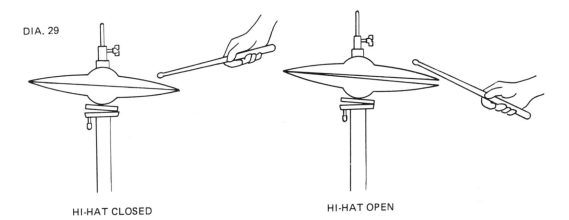

HI-HAT CLOSED   HI-HAT OPEN

The following two pages involve the open and closed hi-hat with the snare drum added.

The tail of the snare drum note ♩ is now placed under the head ⸜ to allow the hi-hat rhythm to be included in the part.

The snare drum is usually placed on the 2nd and 4th beats. This is known as the off-beat or back-beat.

Bass drum patterns with single beats.

Bass drum and snare drum notation tied together.

Semi-quaver exercises played with one stick on hi-hat, snare drum off-beat and semi-quaver bass drum accents.

Double handed exercises played with both sticks on hi-hat.

DIA. 30

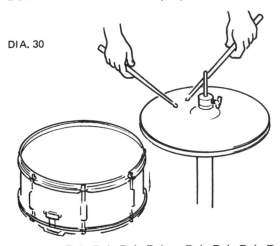

Fast tempos need both sticks on the hi-hat with snare drum accents played among the hi-hat rhythms for continuity.

Rock Fill-ins

Below are a few Rock fills for a full drum outfit.

Begin each exercise with one bar of time or rhythm.

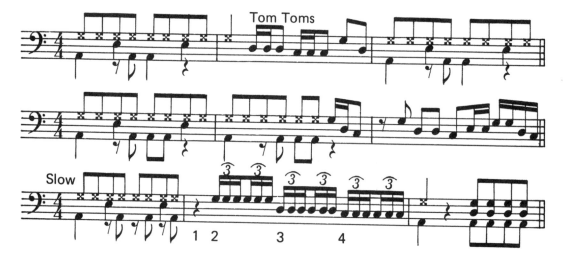

When the sign 'fill-in' is written on drum music, play your own ad lib rhythm to suit each tune.

Example Drum Parts
Shuffle or Boogie

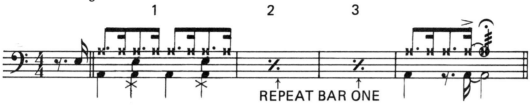
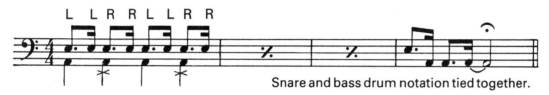

REPEAT BAR ONE

Double handed on snare drum

Snare and bass drum notation tied together.

Beguine

Pick up

Different notation for same effect.

or

Waltz with brushes or sticks.

Brushes

The brushes consist of wire or plastic strands bound together. They are very flexible and capable of producing a variety of effects and sounds.

No standard notation is used for brushes. The word 'brushes', B.R. or W.B. (wire brushes) is used in drum parts to indicate when to use them.

The movement of the hands is very important to achieve a swinging feel. A sweep

across the drum head is usually indicated with a tie.

Use a very simple brush rhythm for swinging the group or orchestra along.

Start with the left brush on the left hand side of the batter head and swish over to the right (Fig. 1).

The return swish falls on the second beat (Fig. 2).

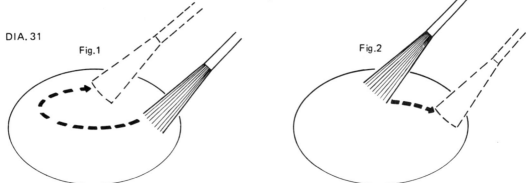

DIA. 31

Fig. 1

Fig. 2

Swish from the second beat on the left (Fig. 3) over to the right for the third beat, and return to the left for the fourth beat (Fig. 4).

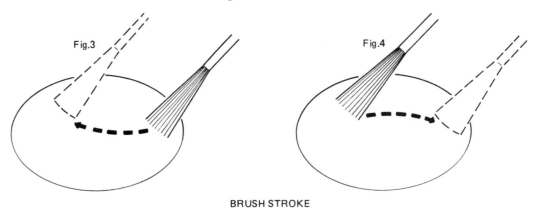

Fig. 3

Fig. 4

BRUSH STROKE

With the left hand above supplying the swish, the right hand now plays the time or rhythm.

Brushes are effective for soft playing and may be used instead of sticks for Latin rhythms.

To simulate the sound of a shaker or cabasa, make short sweeps across the head in eighth notes. Play a stick across the rim with your other hand for a basic clave beat.

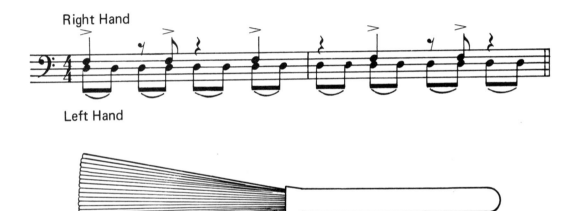

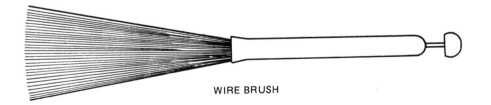

NYLON BRUSH

WIRE BRUSH

DIA. 32

Advanced Reading Exercises for the Snare Drum

Exercise 1 has accented tied notes. It is therefore in syncopated form — the stress being away from the normal pulse (the note at the end of each tie is *not* struck).

(1)

mf (at a steady blues tempo)

An exercise in **3/4** time with strong accents. R L or L R throughout.

(2)

f

58

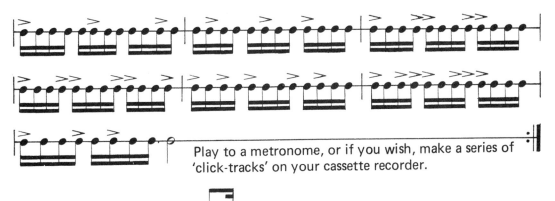

Play to a metronome, or if you wish, make a series of 'click-tracks' on your cassette recorder.

Exercise 3 has dotted rhythms. ♪. ♩ etc.

To feel this dotted rhythm correctly, play the strokes on the crosses with one stick striking the drum and the other striking your knee or in the air.

etc.

R L L R R L L R
or L R R L L R R L

(3) ♩ = 60

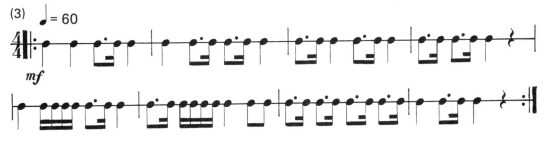

mf

Exercise 4 is as Exercise 3 but in $\frac{2}{4}$ time. Make certain the dotted rhythms *are* dotted. They must not sound as parts of triplets, or in the time of $\frac{6}{8}$

(4) ♩ = 120

Don't let this exercise beat you. *You 'beat' it.*

An exercise using the compound rhythms of $\frac{6}{8}$, $\frac{9}{8}$, and $\frac{12}{8}$, and the occasionally used $\frac{15}{8}$. Play all the grace notes quietly and neatly.

LR or
RL

LLR or
RRL

LRLR or
RLRL

60

In Exercise 6 make certain the quaver triplets (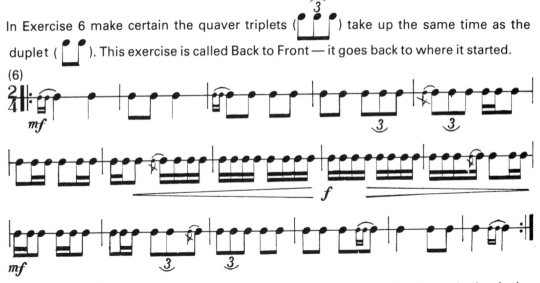) take up the same time as the duplet ( ). This exercise is called Back to Front — it goes back to where it started.

(6)

An exercise in $\frac{5}{4}$ time. The first two bars are based on the relentless drum rhythm in the movement *Mars, the Bringer of War,* from the Suite, *The Planets* by Gustav Holst.

(7)

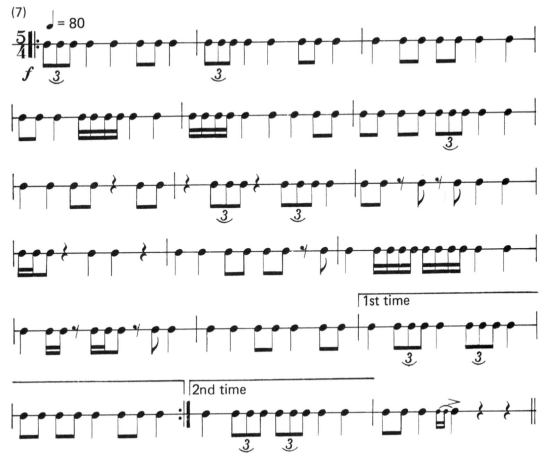

1st time

2nd time

From here to there

(8)

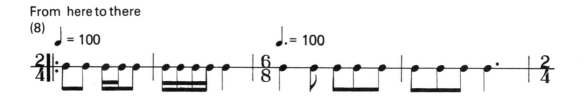

On the rim · **Rim shots**

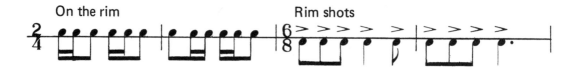

Rim · **Click sticks**

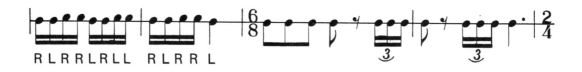

R L R R L R L L   R L R R   L

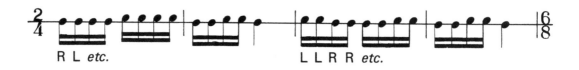

R L *etc.* · L L R R *etc.*

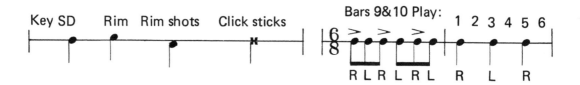

Key SD   Rim   Rim shots   Click sticks   Bars 9&10 Play: 1 2 3 4 5 6

R L R L R L   R   L   R

The snare drum part from the finale of the famous overture *Pique Dame* by Suppe.

The snare drum, bass drum and cymbals part of *Pique Dame* overture as played 'double-drumming'. The bass drum and snare drum are struck simultaneously when written so. The foot cymbals were played closed or open as written and all grace notes on the snare drum were played.

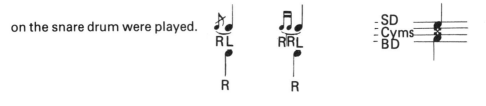

(10)

The Percussion Instruments of the Latin-American Orchestra

Latin-American percussion is now used in many kinds of music, including jazz, rock, disco, movie and TV shows, and symphonic works. To know about these instruments is valuable, and to be able to play them is not only an aid to modern kit technique, but essential to the modern drummer. There are a great number of Latin-American instruments and they are all fun to play. Chief among them are: maracas, claves, scrapers, tambourines, cowbells, timbales and conga drums.

Though the Latin-American orchestra is a modern musical ensemble, many of the instruments that are such a feature in a Latin-American rhythm section have a long history. Rattles (maracas) were one of the first instruments used by ancient people. Nature almost formed them for these early people, for these primitive instruments were merely pods of plants in which the seeds had dried. Rattles were mainly used as rhythm providers for dancing. They were also supposed to have magical powers. Witch doctors used them when they prayed for rain and tried to disperse evil spirits.

Bongos, timbales, and congas, are elaborate models of the skin drums used in olden times. Today these remarkable percussion instruments are the very heart of Latin-American music. Other instruments adding exotic rhythms to Latin-American music include the talking drum, cuica, vibra-slap, cowbells, triangle and cabasa. You will find the form of the Latin-American percussion instruments and the way to play them clearly explained. The catchy rhythms are not only fascinating and fun to play, they also stimulate your interest and drum technique, and add to your performance on the drum kit, and on any other type of percussion instruments that may appeal to you.

Tambourine

Tambourines which are strongly associated with Spanish music and many kinds of folk music, can be traced to the early days of music making. They are mentioned in the opening chapters of the Bible. Today, tambourines add fascinating rhythms and local colour, not only to the Latin-American orchestra, but to many other kinds of music.

Tambourine with Head or Skin

The tambourine is held in the hand between the thumb and the finger tips. It is struck by the fingers of your other hand. In soft passages only the outside rim of the tambourine needs to be tapped.

If the head is tapped very softly, a tom tom sound will be produced without the jingle effects.

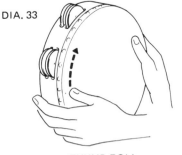

DIA. 33

THUMB ROLL

For very loud passages the player may strike the head with the knuckles.

The thumb roll (Dia. 33) requires practice. Hold the tambourine loosely and with your other hand rub your thumb round the edge of the skin. Your thumb needs a little moisture on it or alternatively try rubbing some resin on the edge of the head.

Example

Bars one and two require you to tap on the edge of the tambourine, bars three and four are thumb rolls and bars five and six require accents from your knuckles.

The normal roll is achieved by shaking the tambourine from side to side.

When playing the rock tambourine without a head, we shake the tambourine from side to side and tap the heel of the other hand on to the tambourine shell to make the accent.

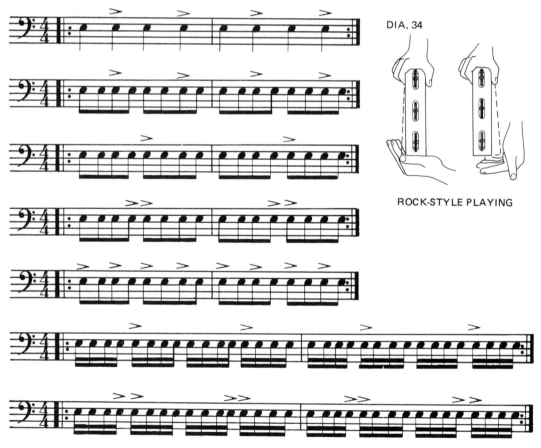

DIA. 34

ROCK-STYLE PLAYING

Claves

Claves (rhythm sticks) have been used as rhythm providers over a long period of time. In the harvest fields of ancient Egypt, claves (known as concussion sticks) were used as timekeepers. The claves were played by lady musicians who gave a steady beat which helped the men to swing their scythes in rhythm.

To achieve the important hollow sound from the claves, one hand is cupped holding the first clave between the finger tips and thumb.

The second clave is held like a drum stick, striking the first clave in the centre.

Both claves must be held loosely, so the wood gives a ringing sound. Holding the claves tightly will only dampen the sound.

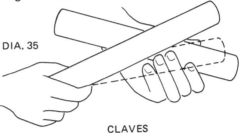

DIA. 35

CLAVES

Example of Notation

Basic Clave Beat

Bossa Nova

Variations

67

Triangle

The triangle is one of the most used of all the small hand held instruments. There is no substitute for this sound. A bell or cymbal will not be a satisfactory replacement.

The tone from the triangle should be high pitched, with a good silvery open ringing sound.
A good supply of triangle beaters is necessary for soft or loud sounds.

The triangle is held either by a clip fixed to a music stand, or by the finger through a loop of string or gut (Dia. 36).

DIA. 36

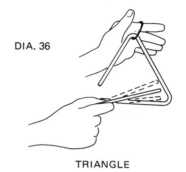

TRIANGLE

The Roll or Trill

Hold the beater in one of the two closed corners of the triangle and strike from side to side. Keep the triangle open and ringing.

When suspending the triangle from a music stand by a clip, always check to see everything is set in a manner that will not permit the stand to topple over.

Also check that the triangle will not spin around when it is struck. Adjust the gut or string if necessary.

To play a rhythm pattern on the triangle place one finger through the loop of gut or string and close the hand over the triangle for a closed sound. Leave the hand open for an open or ringing sound.

Closed sound ✗   Open sound ⊗

Try to vary the sound from the triangle by striking each of the three sides.

The triangle should sound for the exact value of the note written.

Guiro (or Scraper)

Scrapers (the guiro and reso-reso) were used in much the same way as rattles. Scrapers were thought to have supernatural powers. At the sowing of the seed in the Far East, scrapers were used in the prayers for a fruitful harvest.

Holding the guiro in one hand, the stick or wire prong is scraped or tapped along its ridges with the other hand. To play crotchets or quarter notes, scrape the entire length of the guiro. For quavers or eighth notes, scrape up and down, playing two scrapes in the time of one. The scrape sound is also notated with a tie.

DIA. 37

GUIRO

Tamborim

The tamborim is a small hand drum without jingles. The instrument is held in the left hand while the right hand strikes it with a drumstick on the skin or rim.

The left hand also applies pressure under the skin, to raise or lower the pitch.

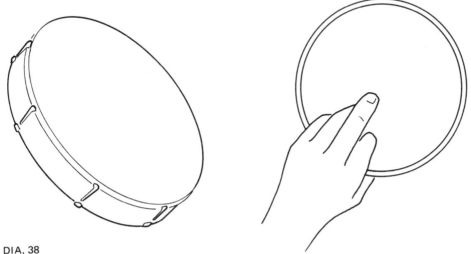

DIA. 38

TAMBORIM

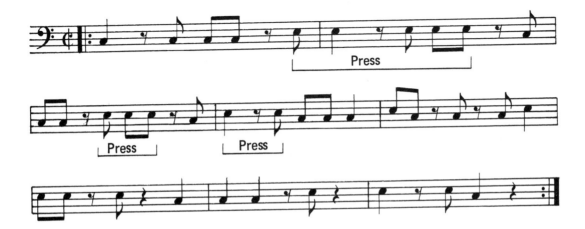

Afuche (Metal Cabasa)

DIA. 39

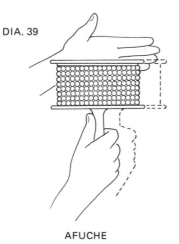

AFUCHE

The Afuche is held in the right hand with the left hand resting on the rotating beads.

Twist the cylinder both ways in even time. Accents are made by pressing your left hand on the beads.

A roll may be achieved by shaking the afuche with one hand.

Cuica

The Cuica shell is made of wood or metal, with a calf skin drum head tensioned on one end of the shell. A cane is attached to a small ball which is sewn into the centre of the drum head.

The player holds the shell of the Cuica with one hand. This hand also applies pressure to the head or skin. Fig. 1.

Very high notes are made by pressing hard on the head.

Place a small damp cloth on to the cane and by rubbing the cloth up and down the cane, the player vibrates the head. Fig. 2.

Fig.2

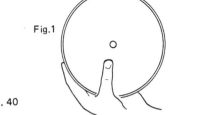

Fig.1

DIA. 40

CUICA

Example of Cuica Rhythm

High pressure. | Gliss (Slide up or down the cane).

Timbales

Timbales are single headed drums made from brass or stainless steel. The shells are open at the bottom and have calf or plastic heads on top.

Timbale sticks made from thin dowel are used.

Regular snare drum sticks are generally too heavy.

The 'Paila' sound is achieved by playing on the outside of each shell (Dia. 41).

DIA. 41

TIMBALES

Shells made from metal produce a live ringing sound. To dampen this sound press the sticks against the shells.

The 'Paila' sound is used with occasional fills played on the heads of the timbales.

You may wish to ad lib at the end of the phrases — be sure this is done tastefully.

Cow bells are used with timbales. These are fixed to a cow bell post attached to the timbale stand.

Vibra Slap

VIBRASLAP

The vibra slap is used more for effect than for playing rhythms. It now takes the place of a jaw bone (Quijada).

The vibra slap is held by the metal handle with one hand. The other hand hits the wooden ball, allowing the steel pins to vibrate in the sound box.

76

Cabasa

The handle of the cabasa is held in the right hand. The beads of the instrument rest on the palm of the left hand. A twisting movement is made with the right hand, which rotates the shell, while the beads stay in the same position on the palm of the left hand.

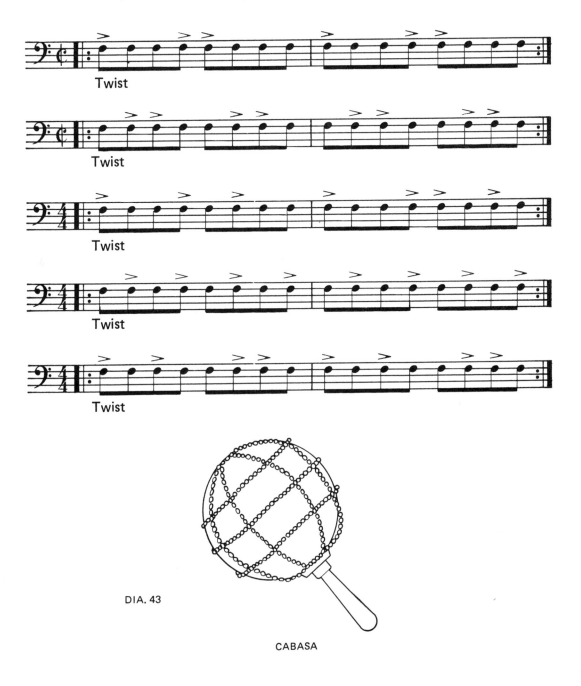

DIA. 43

CABASA

Cowbells (hand held)

The hand held cowbell may be used in many rhythms, from 4 in a bar for rock numbers to open and closed sounds for various Latin-American percussion rhythms.

The cowbell in Latin-American groups plays a straight beat and holds and controls the tempo for other Latin instruments with more difficult rhythms.

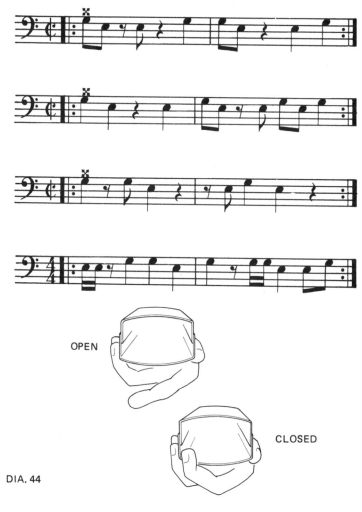

OPEN

CLOSED

DIA. 44

COWBELL

Hold the cowbell in the palm of the hand. Strike it with a thick dowel or the butt end of a drum stick. For a low sound strike the lip or edge of the cowbell. Striking it on the top or side will produce a high sound.

The open sound (Figure 1) may be controlled by your hand to produced a closed sound (Figure 2).

Maracas

The maracas are played with a backwards and forwards movement. The rhythm of the maracas is a constantly pulsating one. To play a roll, the maracas can be swirled in a circular motion.

R L R L R L R L R L   R L R L R L R L R L

R L R L L L R R   R L R L L L R R

For finger style playing, hold a maraca in each hand and tap the top of the instrument with the index fingers.

DIA. 45

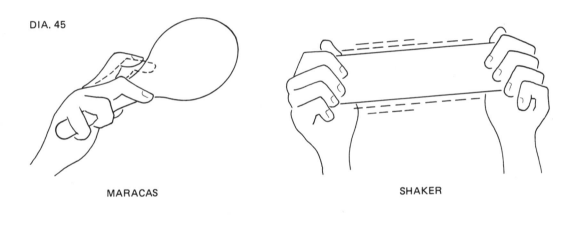

MARACAS   SHAKER

R L R L R L R L R   R L R L R L R L R

R L R L R R L L R L R L R R L L   R L R L R R L L R L R L R R L L

Shaker (Chocalho)

The shaker is played with a forward and backward movement from the elbow.

Make sure the accents can be heard.

The more vigorous the arm movement, the louder the accent.

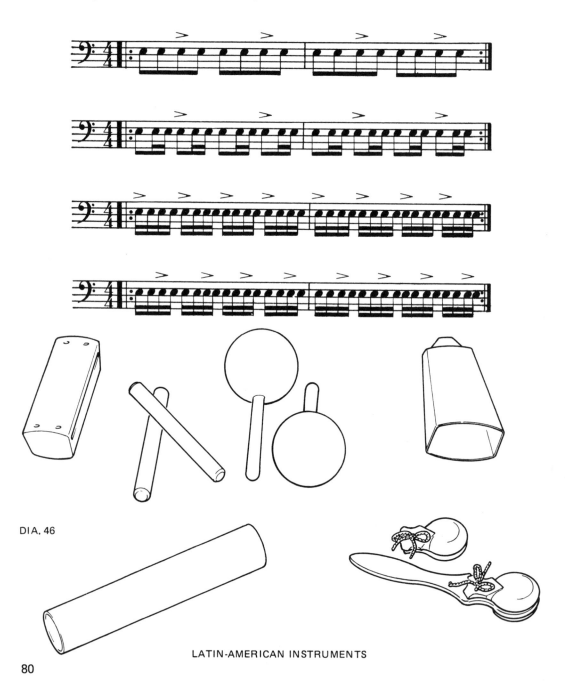

DIA. 46

LATIN-AMERICAN INSTRUMENTS

Agogo Bells

The bells are joined together with a handle. They are usually of a high and low pitch and are played with a mallet of wood, metal or soft material.

DIA. 47

AGOGO BELLS

The bells may have a flexible handle which allows them to come into contact with each other.

Wooden Agogos

Played with a wooden mallet (timbale stick) two tones are produced. High and low guiro sounds are achieved by rubbing the stick across the grooves.

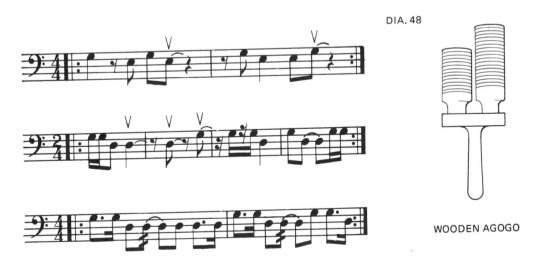

DIA. 48

WOODEN AGOGO

Bongos

The player sits with the bongos held between the knees, with the small drum positioned to the player's left. The middle three fingers are used, the first and second fingers doing most of the playing. Strike with the finger tips near the edge of each drum with a snapping wrist movement.

Four-Stroke Finger Rolls

Start with the little finger and bring the other fingers down sharply on to the drum head.

Conga Drums

The conga drums have a much deeper sound than bongos and are played with a more basic rhythm.

Holding one conga between the knees in a sitting position, make sure one side of the conga shell is a couple of inches off the floor. With the drum tilted, the pitch is low.

CONGAS

DIA. 49

Variations in the way the conga drums are played will produce a wide range of sounds.

The slap sound is produced by hitting the head and rim of the drum simultaneously, while the other hand presses the head down, producing a higher pitched ringing sound.

Open Closed

83

Other Hand Held Instruments

Castanets

These are held by a cord looped round the thumb and played with the fingers. Sometimes they are mounted on handles and shaken. A castanet machine is used today for ease of playing (Dia. 50).

DIA. 50

CASTANET MACHINE

The castanets are mounted on a wooden block. The sound is produced by tapping on top of each castanet with your fingers.

Finger Cymbals

Made from brass or bronze, the small cymbals are struck together to produce a high pitched bell-like sound.

Flexatone

This instrument, often heard in cartoon music and films is a thin flexible plate on a small frame, with two beaters attached to the frame. The pitch is varied by thumb pressure on the plate.

Mark Tree

This instrument is used for a glissando effect, similar to the sound of wind chimes. Made from thin brass tubes of graduated lengths, the mark tree may be played with your fingers or a brass mallet.

Ratchet

The sound is like a football rattle. It is played continuously by winding a handle attached to a cog, or wound at intervals for rhythmic effects.

Sandpaper blocks

Wooden blocks with sandpaper attached and used for special effects. May be played like a shaker rhythm for very quiet rhythm passages.

Sleigh Bells

Small round bells attached to a leather strap or wooden handle.

Talking Drum (Kalengo)

The player holds the drum under his arm and squeezes the cords on the drum for a change of pitch. The other hand strikes the drum with a curved mallet.

Whip or Slapstick

Two thin pieces of wood hinged at one end. The effect is similar to a crack of a whip. Sometimes used in commercial recording for back beat punctuation.

Woodblock

Rectangular woodblock used for many effects as an accessory with the drum outfit.

Temple Blocks or Skulls

Lower in pitch than the woodblock and used in sets of two or more different sizes. A variety of tones can be produced by using hard, medium or soft mallets.

How to play Orchestral Percussion

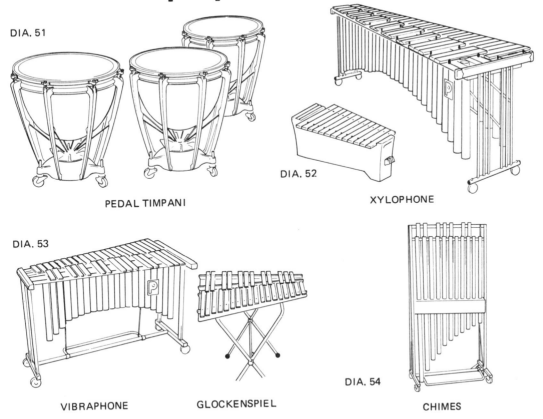

DIA. 51

PEDAL TIMPANI

DIA. 52

XYLOPHONE

DIA. 53

VIBRAPHONE

GLOCKENSPIEL

DIA. 54

CHIMES

The object of this chapter is to give you a broad view of the percussion instruments involved in the orchestral repertoire, and those used in schools; to deal briefly with their history and the important part they play in many kinds of music, and to outline the basic approach to orchestral techniques by means of progressive exercises and interesting examples.

Of the many percussion instruments that play a vital part in the orchestra and school groups, the timpani are generally considered to be the most important in a modern orchestral percussion section. The timpani were also the first percussion instruments to be used by the great composers of the past.

Timpani are noble instruments with a romantic history. Originally they were cavalry kettledrums*used in pairs mounted one on each side of the drum horse's back, and played by a mounted kettledrummer who was a very important and skilful man who kept his special art a great secret. At one time only royal persons were allowed to have kettledrummers. These mounted kettledrums were highly esteemed instruments. In battle they were considered (like the flag) a prize of war. The army which captured the kettledrums or flag was immediately the victor.

* Mounted kettledrums are still used in one or two British regiments.

Around the year 1700 great orchestral composers like Purcell, Bach and Handel, began to write music for kettledrums, and cavalry drums were then allowed to be used in orchestras, where in most cases they accompanied the trumpets.

At the time of these early composers the kettledrums were smaller than the timpani we know today. The large drum of a pair measured around 23" in diameter, and the small drum 21" across. These small drums had calfskin heads which could be tuned to different notes by tensioning screws, so composers were able to write for two notes (high and low) which sounded in the bass clef — like the low notes of a piano. Due to the limited musical range of these cavalry drums the notes most often used at that time were the strong notes (the tonic and dominant) of the trumpeters' keys of C and D. The

tuning for the key of C was and the tuning for the key of D

the intervals in each case being a fourth, with the dominant note below the tonic note. As time went on larger kettledrums with an extended compass were made. Another advance was that three or more drums were used in orchestras. This allowed composers to write for more notes than the tonic and dominant, and to use

extended intervals such as a fifth with the dominant above the tonic or at times

an octave.

Eventually tuning mechanism was improved and in course of time orchestral timpani with pedal tuning were invented. Pedal-tuned timpani are used in all modern orchestras and bands, and in time will be used in the schools which at present have only hand-screw timpani, though it must be said that a great deal can be done with hand-screw drums, and much can be learned from their use as preparatory instruments.

Orchestral Timpani

(Eng. kettledrums; Fr. timbales; Ger. Pauken; It. timpani — timpani is plural, timpano is singular.)

Modern timpani consist of copper or fibre-glass bowls with a single head of plastic or calfskin. Plastic heads are normally used and are recommended as they are only slightly affected by atmospheric changes. Timpani with copper bowls are used in most orchestras because of their tone quality, but fibre-glass bowls (which are cheaper) are useful in schools for reason of their durability.

There are several types of orchestral timpani. The most usual are those that are swiftly tuned by foot pedal mechanism, and those that are hand tuned. Most pedal-tuned timpani are fitted with tuning gauges with pointers which, if correctly set, indicate the note to which the drum is tuned. Indicators are very useful when playing modern music with many changes of tuning, *but remember* your ear should be the deciding factor when tuning (see tuning exercises).

The Instruments

Hand-screw timpani are tuned by turning the handles clockwise to raise the pitch and, in the opposite way to release the pressure, which lowers the pitch. Pedal timpani are more quickly tuned by means of the foot-pedal mechanism.

The musical compass of an orchestral timpano is from five to seven full tones and great care must be taken when tuning to a high note. If the drumhead is too tightly tensioned it has little musical value and may also be damaged. The chart below gives the sizes and ranges of a set of 5 orchestral timpani and the diameters and compass of a pair of standard timpani (such as those often used in schools).* Note that the large drums are to the left of the player and that they are arranged in the form of a crescent, giving the bass sounds to the left, as are the notes of a xylophone, etc. (The drum kit toms are arranged differently and you may notice that some Continental timpanists play with the large drums to the right.)

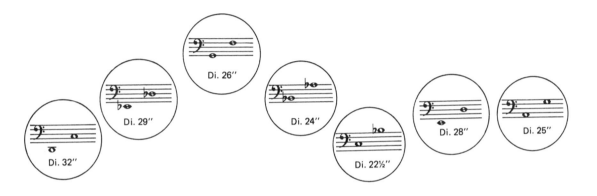

Timpani Sticks

At least four pairs of sticks of graded texture are necessary: soft; medium; hard felt and wooden-ended. Very soft sticks produce a beautiful tone, but are less articulate than harder sticks. Composers occasionally state the type of sticks required, otherwise the character of the written part suggests the grade to be used. An ideal stick is one with a core of balsa wood or cork, covered with piano damper felt.

The sticks are held in the matched grip, i.e. with the thumb and index finger gripping the shaft in each hand, and the second and third fingers acting as a cushion with the palms facing downwards. The shafts of the sticks should be held a little below the point of balance (towards the plain end).

*These ranges are reliant upon the drum and the drumhead being in good condition.

Technical Approach and Tone Production

Facility and tone production on the timpani are acquired by way of basic exercises commencing with the approach to the roll. The roll on the timpani is as the single stroke roll on the snare drum, bearing in mind that regularity and uniformity of tone are more important in the initial stages than speed, and that too rapid a roll will tend to choke the vibrations of the drumhead.

The drumhead is struck with a swift movement of the drumstick, at the playing spot which is approximately three inches from the rim. To avoid stifling the tone the stick must be withdrawn from the drumhead *immediately*. Another important factor in tone production is that the drumhead is tensioned evenly with the head sounding the same pitch at all tensioning points. Rolls of varying weights and differing dynamic markings require different techniques. A pp roll may be played a little towards the rim. For a fp roll allow a fractional wait after the initial blow before beginning the roll. An important aspect of sound production in timpani playing is the observance by tone control of note values. A well-tuned kettledrum, if it is correctly struck, has a long period of sound. Where necessary, the ringing tone of the drum should be silenced, as quietly as possible, by 'damping' the vibrating drumhead with the fingers. In some cases it is necessary to place a small felt pad on the drumhead to clarify certain passages. The further the pad is placed from the playing area the shorter the length of the sound:

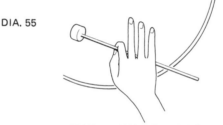

DIA. 55

TIMPANI-HAND DAMPING

Tuning

What is required from a timpanist as well as a good technique is good intonation. Practice will develop good technique. Care and concentration on the following tuning routine will train your ear to tune correctly.

Tuning Routines

Listen to the note C taken from a fixed pitch instrument such as a pitch pipe or a C tuning fork. Now sing or hum that note, then sing down the scale (in tonic sol-fa) from

the note C to the note G calling the notes in your mind—doh, te, lah, soh.

Now sing only the notes C and G, the interval of a fourth and the tonic and dominant

notes of the key of C with the dominant below the tonic.   Next sing *up* the

scale from C to G calling the notes in your mind — doh, ray, me, fah, soh, and then sing only the C and G, the interval of a *fifth* with the dominant *above* the tonic.

Now learn to sing these two intervals in other keys as they are the most used and the most important intervals in music for the timpani. If your ear is at all sluggish you will find that practising these tuning routines will greatly improve your sense of pitch. When you can sing in tune the intervals of a fourth and fifth in several keys, you will cope well with the other intervals used in music for the timpani.*

You must now accustom your ear to the sound of orchestral timpani as they sound in the bass clef, and are always written in that clef. First tune a pair of drums to the notes C and G, with the dominant below the tonic. Sing the note C and tune that note first. Then tune the larger drum to G. Strike the drums at the playing spot and then make certain you sing the notes you have tuned on the drums. Now tune your small drum to the note D and you will have the tonic and dominant of the key of G with the dominant in this case *above* the tonic. Having tuned to a lower and upper dominant practise tuning in other keys, and always tune quietly as if you were playing in an orchestra. Test the pitch with a quiet flick of the finger or drumstick with your ear close to the drumhead. Another test for pitch and true resonance is to hum the note you want into the playing spot, and if necessary adjust the pitch of the drum until you hear the note 'singing' back to you. Make certain that the drum is tuned evenly all round.

Tuning Exercises

You will find, for example, that (due to the limited compass of a pair of standard timpani) in the key of Ab the dominant note can only be placed above the tonic note, and in the key of Eb the dominant must be below the tonic. With a set of symphonic drums, composers can write for upper and lower dominants in all keys (see chart).

Technical Exercises and Examples from the Standard Repertoire

Alternate beating where practicable is the general rule in timpani playing. There are however numerous occasions when alternate beating is *not* practicable. The following technical exercises should be practised to develop alternate beating, alternative beatings, double beatings and cross-overs. Play all exercises at the same tempo. Do not accelerate *during* an exercise and play all at various dynamic levels.

*Some people can sing any note at will; this is known as perfect pitch.

For practice purposes many of these exercises can be played on kit toms or unsnared snare drum by positioning the floor tom to the left.

Duples etc. (evens) using 'singles'. Start with the left — the inside hand.

(1)   In D & A

Duples etc. (evens) with cross-overs. Start on the right — the outside hand.

(2)

Triples (odds) using singles. Start with the outside hand.

(3)

Triples with cross-overs, with the start on the inside hand.

(4)

You will see from the above exercises that when evens start on the inside hand and odds on the outside hand, no cross-overs are used.

Exercise 5 starts with the outside hand and uses cross-overs. Cross-overs are spectacular and interesting to play, but occasions occur when it is not advisable to use a cross-over, as the swing of the stick may add weight to the stroke or result in the drum head being struck in the wrong place.

Exercise 6 is the same as Exercise 5 but using double beats and paradiddle to avoid cross-overs.

(5)

R L R L etc.

L R L R etc.

(6)

L R L L RLRRLRLL RLRRLRLL RLRRL

L R L L R R L R L L R L R R L R L L R L R R L R L L R

An example to be played on three drums using the paradiddle to avoid a long cross-over from the high drum to the low drum. If using timpani tune to If using kit toms or practice pads arrange accordingly.

(7) Timpani in G — C -- E

R L R L R L R R L R L L etc.

R L R L etc.   R L R R L R L L R L R R   L R L L R L R R L

Practise this exercise for playing cross-overs. Cross the stick *over* with a swift gliding movement and avoid clicking the sticks together or striking the drumhead clumsily or catching the rim of the drum as you swing over.

A march theme written for a pair of drums using tied and untied rolls and 'damping'. Practise starting and finishing the rolls on either hand.

Assembly

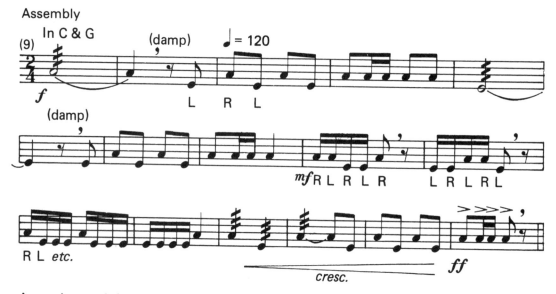

A stately march for three drums. Go back to the basic beatings and work out your own sticking routine. 'Damp' where you feel necessary.

Fine

Orchestral Repertoire

Example 11 is from Purcell's opera *The Fairy Queen* which was written in 1692. The passage is solo, and is considered to be the first solo ever written for orchestral timpani. Note the drums are tuned to D & A (the key of D — one of the early keys used by trumpeters), and that Purcell calls the timpani by their English name: kettledrums.

(11) Kettledrums (Purcell)

This example is typical of Handel's scoring for the timpani.

(12) Alexander's Feast (Handel)

This entry on the timpani comes when the choir sing 'Rouse him like a peal of thunder'.

Example 13 with the drums tuned in octaves is from Beethoven's Ninth Symphony (1826). In concert performances it is played at a very fast speed. Molto vivace ♩.= 116.

(13) Ninth Symphony (Beethoven)

Example 14 is the melodic passage (solo) from the score of the opera *Robert le Diable* written by the French composer Meyerbeer in 1831.

(14) Robert le Diable (Meyerbeer)

In these two examples from Saint-Saëns *Samson and Delilah* tune two drums to A and E and in the 6 bars' rest hum the note D and change the E to D

Make the change as quickly and as quietly as possible and practise pitch changes. This could prepare you for orchestral playing in which there are so often many changes of pitch, often to be made in a short time.

(15) Samson and Delilah (Saint-Saëns)

This passage for 3 timpani is from the Fourth Symphony by Tchaikovsky. Note carefully the time signature ($\frac{9}{8}$), the dotted notes and the L.R. etc.

Fourth Symphony (Tschaikovsky)

These short examples from well-known standard works were written by great composers of the past, who did so much to explore the possibilities of orchestral timpani.

94

Looking at an Orchestral Timpanist's Part

Key signatures are rarely given in music for the timpani — composers normally state the notes required.

The glissandi in section (B) are only possible on pedal-tuned drums. The pitch, as here written, is raised by pressure on the foot-pedal from the F♯ until the drum sounds the B♮ and in bar 17 of section (B) the B♮ drum is quickly lowered to F♯. In bar 21 the rise and fall is as written. In bar 32 of the section (C) the trumpet cue is given as a guide for the timpanist.

The Tuned Percussion

Orchestral percussion is divided into three groups: the timpani which, with their notes of definite pitch, enter into the harmony of the orchestra; the instruments of indefinite musical pitch (the snare drum, etc.); and the group known as the tuned percussion which includes the xylophone, glockenspiel, vibraphone, marimba and tubular bells (chimes). Though the purpose and tone of these instruments differ considerably, the technical approach to them all is similar, and a good performance on one (for example the xylophone) will lead to a good performance on them all.

The Xylophone (meaning 'wood sound')

Xylophones, like many other percussion instruments have been traced to the early days of music making. The first xylophones we know of were made from pieces of tree branch of different length which were laid across the shins of a seated player. To give the bars a more resonant sound a pit was dug between the legs of the player. This primitive instrument developed into the log xylophone with wooden logs of different length loosely laid over a deep pit. A further step came with the xylophones used in Asia over a thousand years ago. These were trough resonated with the bars of wood laid across a resonance box. Trough-resonated metallophones were also used in Asia at this early period; they were bronze adaptations of the xylophones. (This early method of adding resonance is with us today in the xylophones and metallophones used in primary schools.)

Xylophones were also being used in other countries, particularly in Africa, where 16th-century explorers found elaborate instruments which they reported the natives played with amazing skill. The bars of these African xylophones were arranged (as the Asian instrument) in a single row. The tone of each bar was amplified by being suspended over a gourd resonator with air column content corresponding to the pitch of the bar above. The large deep-sounding instruments were known as marimbas, and our present orchestral tube-resonated xylophones and marimbas are, in principle, scientific copies of these early instruments.

In Europe, xylophones were used at least five hundred years ago. They were not as highly developed as the instruments used in Asia and Africa. They were in fact merely tuned wooden bars laid across ropes of straw. One early European 16th-century musicologist called the xylophone of his day *hultze glechter* (wooden clatter). By the end of the 19th century the xylophone had become an orchestral instrument. It was used effectively as such by the French composer Saint-Saëns who wrote for it in his *Danse Macabre* to imitate skeleton's bones, and later to represent fossils in *The Carnival of Animals.* Modern composers make many uses of the various tonal effects that are possible on our rich sounding xylophones and marimbas.

The Orchestral Xylophone

Xylophones and glockenspiels etc. are known as 'keyboards', and a knowledge of the keyboard and key signatures is the first step to good performance. The bars of an orchestral xylophone and other tuned percussion instruments are arranged in two rows, in the manner of the piano keyboard with the low notes to the left. The front and back rows of bars correspond to the white and black notes of the piano. To facilitate the playing of fast passages the back row of notes is usually raised on an orchestral xylophone. The bars are made from a durable wood such as rosewood, or from a synthetic material called kelon. The compass of orchestral xylophones varies from two and a half to four octaves — a four octave xylophone sounding from middle C on the piano to four octaves above. The music for the xylophone is written in the treble clef, either at true pitch or (more often), an octave lower than the instrument actually sounds (see glockenspiel). Another popular orchestral xylophone has a range of 3½ octaves, with the lowest note sounding F above middle C. For the exercises and melodies to follow, an instrument with at least three octaves is required.

Diagram 56 gives the range and the formation of the notes of a 3 octave xylophone. The names of the notes are given, but they are not always imprinted on the bars of an orchestral instrument.

DIA. 56

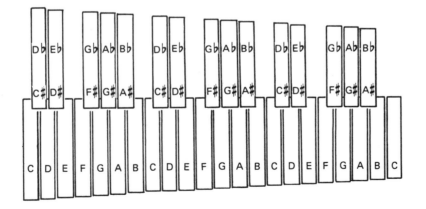

You will notice that C sharp is also called D flat and, for example, G sharp is also called A flat. The notes in the back row are sometimes called accidentals. It is not strictly correct to describe them so as they are *not* accidentals in certain keys. (See key signatures.)

If you play the piano or are learning to do so, the keyboard layout will be familiar to you. If you are not familiar with the keyboard, study its formation, as this will make the basic exercises and the playing of tunes so understandable and enjoyable.

As your drumming technique will give you facility on all tuned percussion instruments, the next step is to become acquainted with the way the music for the xylophone is written and how it is governed by key signatures. There are many key signatures, but a fair knowledge of the five signatures used in this chapter will serve as a springboard and give you the form of other key signatures. The examples are in the treble clef (𝄞) which is the clef in which the music for the xylophone is written. The five keys used as examples are as follows:

The key of C (the open key). This key has *no* flats or sharps

The key of F. This key has *one* flat (B flat)

The key of B flat has *two* flats   (B♭ and E♭)

The key of G. This key has *one* sharp (F sharp)

The key of D has *two* sharps   (F♯ and C♯)

(Find these notes on the keyboard chart.)

Note the flats and sharps which signify the key are always placed at the beginning of a given section, and that they follow the clef sign and precede the time signature.

There is an easy and sure method of remembering the progression of flats and sharps.

Flat keys go up in fourths and the flattened note is always the *fourth* note above the keynote. Sharp keys go up in fifths and the note that is sharpened is always the *seventh* note above the keynote. For example, for the key with one flat, count four

notes *up* from the note C (counting C as one)   and we reach the note F.

Count four notes (a fourth) *up* from the keynote F   and the note B flat is

reached (B flat is given in the key signature). For the key of one sharp, count five

notes (a fifth) *up* from C and we reach G   . To find the note that is sharp-

ened, count *seven* notes *up* from the keynote G   and the note F sharp

is reached (this note is sharpened, as F♯ is given in the key signature). All keys progress in this order — *flat keys in fourths and sharp keys in fifths.* Look back at the key signatures in the keys of C, F, Bb and G and D.

Keyboard Techniques

The beaters. For all-round purposes at least four types of beater are required:

(1) with hard ends (plastic or wood); (2) with ends of vulcanized rubber; (3) with medium rubber ends; (4) with ends of soft rubber or medium hard felt (beaters with softish ends are useful for practice purposes). The ends (maximum one inch in diameter) are best mounted on stiffish cane handles which should be 9-12 inches in length. The grip when playing with two beaters is shown in Dia. 57. They are held in the matched grip with the wrist turned inwards and the palm facing downwards. The shaft is held between the thumb and the first joint of the first finger. The second, third and fourth fingers are held clear of the shaft.*

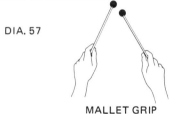

DIA. 57

MALLET GRIP

When playing with two beaters the shafts form an angle of ninety degrees. The stroke is made with a flicking movement of the wrist. The bars are struck in the centre wherever possible, though to facilitate the playing of rapid passages the near ends of the back row notes may be struck. Do *not* strike the bars at the suspension points (the nodal points). The roll on the xylophone is played like a fast single roll on the snare drum.

Basic Exercises and Melodic Examples

The foundation of a good technique on the xylophone and other melodic percussion is built on fluent playing of basic exercises, particularly scales and arpeggios. Make the following exercises your 'daily dozen' and you will soon play the keyboards.

Exercise 1. **The scale of C.** Repeat all examples many times. Aim for correct notes — speed later.

*Four mallet technique is dealt with in the examples for the marimba and vibraphone.

99

A short melody in the key of C. Observe the tied notes and the arpeggio in bar 4. Keep the rhythm strict and mark the accents.

Examples in **the key of F.** Make sure that all B's are flattened as given in the key signature. Note the new rhythm for the scale passage.

An exercise to develop speed and the judgement of distance. (With practice you should soon play this exercise at ♩ = 120 and eventually at ♩ = 160.

Arpeggio with inversions in $\frac{6}{8}$ time.

A march theme in $\frac{6}{8}$ time. Play at a steady tempo $\quad \downarrow. = 80$.

(8)

In all the scale exercises and examples, and those to follow, aim to develop sight-reading. Position the music stand so that both the music and the keyboard can be seen.

The key of G. We move from a flat key to a sharp key. Sharp keys are bright keys and are ideal keys for xylophone music.

(9)

Note how this particular example is formed, and when making the repeat play 8va — one octave higher.

Exercise 10 consists of arpeggios and scale passages. Note the 'sticking' given in bar 3 to avoid a cross-over. Keep an eye on the key signature and the ledger lines.

(10)

Exercise 11 should be played at a brisk tempo. Watch those accidental notes in bars 5, 6, 13 and 14.

'Skiddle-Skaddle'
(11)

A second exercise for developing speed and judging distance.
Are you repeating examples?
(12)

Banks of the Ohio — An American Folk Song

In this melody we use harmony and tied rolls. Tie the rolls over neatly with no accent on the final stroke. To avoid a gap at the end of the tie the harmony note may be omitted Play this tune with softish beaters in the low register of the xylophone.

(13)

(If your xylophone has only three octaves from C upwards, leave out the harmony note B in the last bar.)

The key of B flat. In this scale, note the rhythm and the glissando in the final bar. For the glissando, sweep one beater up the front row of bars and strike the final bar with the other beater.

(14)

(Reminder: are you making *several repeats of the scales* examples?)

Arpeggios in $\frac{9}{8}$ time in the key of Bb.
(15)

In example 16 make a lot of the crescendo and fade away in the last two bars where the rhythm changes.
(16)

This is an exercise to develop double beats with the right and left hand, and for the playing of 'double stops'. Make sure the double notes are struck dead together — there must be no flam effect. Play this piece at a steady tempo.

(17)

(A glissando is an exciting effect on a xylophone *but it must not be used too often.*)

103

The key of D. Scale passages. The octave scale to be repeated without a break.

Make a strong accent on the first beat of each of the bars in $\frac{4}{4}$ time.

(18)

(19) Arpeggios

Eine kleine Nachtmusik (A little Serenade)

This short example is from a famous piece of music written by Mozart. Note the arpeggio in bar 3, and the trill signs in bars 9 and 11. The trills are played as rolls on the written note and the note above, starting and finishing on the lower note.

(20)

This example makes an ideal piece for the glockenspiel.

Further Scales – A Chromatic Scale Starting on C

A chromatic scale goes up and down in semitones. When ascending, the back row notes are written as sharps. Coming down they are written as flats.

(21)

Chromatic scales are fun to play. Play these two examples at a fast speed and then play other chromatic scales starting on different notes.

(22)

(23)

Minor Scales

So far all the scales we have used have been major scales. There are also minor scales, and as all minor scales are the same in formation to know one of them will act as a guide to them all.

Music written in C minor is given the same key signature as the key of E flat major.

The reason for this is that the key of C minor is the relative minor to the key of Eb major. All major keys have a relative minor and this related key is always a minor third (three semitones) below its related major. The important thing to know about a minor scale is that it is in two forms: the harmonic minor and the melodic minor. Both forms are easy to understand and, helpfully, the pattern is the same in all keys.

The Scale of C Minor in Harmonic Form

(24)

This scale goes up and down in the same way. Ascending, the seventh note is raised. The flattened notes are in brackets, as a reminder of the key signature.

The Scale of C Minor in Melodic Form

(25)

The scale of C minor in melodic form goes up one way and comes down in another. Ascending, the sixth and seventh notes are raised, and descending they are flattened as in the key signature. The flats are again bracketed as a reminder.

(Do a little homework on these minor scales — the more you know about music the better you will interpret it.)

The Glockenspiel (Orchestral Bells — U.S.A.)

The sweet bell-like tone of the glockenspiel has coloured orchestral compositions since the middle of the 19th century. It has become one of the most important melodic instruments in the orchestral percussion section. The modern instrument has a

minimum (chromatic) compass of 2½ octaves   It sounds two octaves

higher than normally written, but to avoid the use of upper ledger lines the music is written within the notes given in the diagram.

Hard beaters are normally used on the glockenspiel. Hard rubber beaters are used for special effects, particularly on the lower notes. The metal bars (steel or alloy) should be struck in the centre and always with a swift flicking movement. Any pressure on the bar will deaden the tone.

Orchestral glockenspiels are rarely tube resonated and only specially constructed instruments are equipped with damping mechanism (see vibraphone). Where the sonorous tone of the metal bars overlaps, expert players use a finger damping method as shown in the following examples. To get accustomed to the span of the bars, limber up with a few scales and arpeggios.

An excerpt from *If I were king* overture by Adolphe Adam (1852).

Note the accidentals and the damping cues (𝄾).

(26)

Allegretto

'The entry of the apprentices' — Act 3 *The Mastersingers* overture by Wagner.

(27)

Play the grace notes a shade more open than a flam on the snare drum. Watch the B flats and E flats and the repeats.

The Marimba

The orchestral marimba may be described as a deep toned and mellow sounding xylophone. The concert model has a minimum range of three octaves with the lowest note one octave to one-and-a-quarter octaves below middle C. The lowest note on a bass marimba is two octaves below middle C (in this low register the music is usually written in the bass clef). The marimbas (bass xylophone) used in school ascend from the C below middle C. The instrument called a xylo-rimba is a combination of marimba and xylophone with a compass of four to five octaves.*

The Mallets

Under no circumstances should hard beaters be used on the marimba. In addition to damaging the slender shallow bars, hard beaters rob a marimba of its characteristic sound. Use mallets with long shafts and ends of medium felt, or those with a rubber core covered with yarn, and where possible strike the bars centrally.

Technical Approach

The technical approach to the marimba is that used on the xylophone, and all exercises and examples given for the xylophone can be applied to the marimba. In addition to the two-mallet technique already described, to be really up-to-date with modern marimba playing you should be able to use the four-mallet grip technique. Diagrams 58 and 59 show the normal four-mallet grip which is the same in each hand. One mallet is held between the index finger and the middle finger and the other between the index finger and the thumb. The way the shafts cross over each other in the palm is a matter for personal experiment. The shafts are held together with the third and fourth fingers, and pressure with the thumb and first and second fingers alters, in a scissor-like fashion, the span of the beaters to the required interval.

*With careful use, and storage of the instrument in a moderate temperature, bars of good quality and well-seasoned wood remain well in tune. Any re-tuning (shortening the bar to sharpen and hollowing it to flatten) should be left to a specialist tuner.

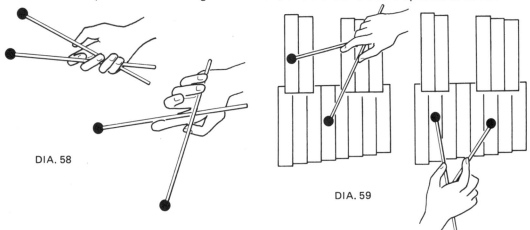

DIA. 58

DIA. 59

With the palms facing downwards (the normal playing position) mentally number the mallets from the left: 1, 2, 3, 4, and place them on the chord of C (C E G C). Mallets 3 and 4 will require a larger span than mallets 1 and 2. Now move all mallets to the notes of the first inversion of the same chord (E G C E). This requires closing the span in the right hand. For the second inversion (G C E G) the span in the left hand must be opened.

108

Now practise on other chords and various intervals, particularly those which include some of the back row of notes. An outward or inward turn of the wrist is determined by the position of the intervals (see Dia. 59).

Strike the ends of the bars if necessary. (See xylophone technique.) Certain chords lie awkwardly if played in one, two, three, four mallet formation. A change of mallet order can be made to avoid an inward turn of both wrists. For example, a diminished 7th chord with C as the lowest note plays comfortably with the mallets positioned as follows:

The methods described are the basics of modern four-hammer technique *on all* melodic percussion instruments.

Exercise 28 — Chord progressions using Dominant 7ths (C7 is the Dominant 7th chord of F). Play the chords with a normal roll. The arpeggios are played with mallets 2 and 3. Tilt mallets 1 and 4 clear of the bars by an inward turn of the wrists and apply a little extra thumb pressure on the mallets 2 and 3.

An exercise for developing the span. Play with a rocking movement.

Four for Fun (Marimba or Xylophone solo)

This piece which is in the key of G is based on three chords: G, D7 and C. Make sure of the F sharps and the various intervals. Play at a steady polka tempo.

The Vibraphone

The vibraphone is the most significant recent addition to the melodic percussion section of the orchestra. It was invented in America in the early part of this century and became, like the marimba, a popular instrument in vaudeville and similar entertainment. By the middle 'twenties the vibraphone had become an important instrument in the dance orchestra. Its unique sound then attracted the attention of serious composers who began to score for it in major compositions. It is now an integral instrument in modern jazz as well as being a prominent instrument in the orchestral percussion section. The compass of the concert model vibraphone is three octaves sounding as written.

In principle the vibraphone is a scientifically constructed tube-resonated metallophone. Revolving discs open and close the upper (open) ends of the resonators and cause the sound from the bars above to emerge in a series of pulsations. The resonant sound of the metal (alloy) bars is controlled by a pedal damper — pressure downwards releasing a felt-covered damper bar. Practice and experience will develop the art of pedal damping, and the occasional use of finger damping.

The Mallets

Vibraphone mallets should have stiff cane shafts, not less than 13″ in length, with yarn-covered tops. The grips are as those used on the marimba.

A Snatch of Jazz
(31)

A Little Prelude by Bach for Vibraphone (or Marimba)
(32)

Damping cues apply to the vibraphone only, and are optional.

Tubular Bells (Orchestral Chimes)

Tubular bells consist of a series of brass (or steel) tubes ranging in diameter from one to two inches. In a standard set of orchestral chimes there are eighteen chromed brass tubes one-and-a-half inches in diameter. The tubes are graduated in length and are arranged in chromatic form in a frame with hand and foot damping mechanism.

The compass is 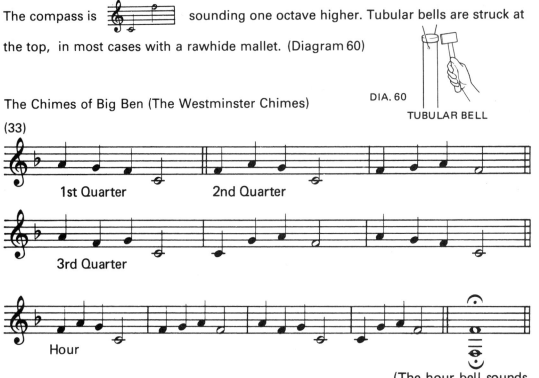 sounding one octave higher. Tubular bells are struck at the top, in most cases with a rawhide mallet. (Diagram 60)

DIA. 60

TUBULAR BELL

The Chimes of Big Ben (The Westminster Chimes)

(33)

1st Quarter 2nd Quarter

3rd Quarter

Hour

(The hour bell sounds one octave lower)

112